A Librarian's Guide on
How to Publish

CHANDOS
INFORMATION PROFESSIONAL SERIES

Series Editor: Ruth Rikowski
(email: Rikowskigr@aol.com)

Chandos' new series of books is aimed at the busy information professional. They have been specially commissioned to provide the reader with an authoritative view of current thinking. They are designed to provide easy-to-read and (most importantly) practical coverage of topics that are of interest to librarians and other information professionals. If you would like a full listing of current and forthcoming titles, please visit our web site www.chandospublishing.com or email info@chandospublishing.com or telephone +44 (0) 1223 499140.

New authors: we are always pleased to receive ideas for new titles; if you would like to write a book for Chandos, please contact Dr Glyn Jones on e-mail gjones@chandospublishing. com or telephone number +44 (0) 1993 848726.

Bulk orders: some organisations buy a number of copies of our books. If you are interested in doing this, we would be pleased to discuss a discount. Please contact on e-mail info@chandospublishing.com or telephone +44 (0) 1223 499140.

A Librarian's Guide on How to Publish

SREĆKO JELUŠIĆ AND IVANKA STRIČEVIĆ

CHANDOS
PUBLISHING

Oxford Cambridge New Delhi

Chandos Publishing
TBAC Business Centre
Avenue 4
Station Lane
Witney
Oxford OX28 4BN
UK
Tel: +44 (0) 1993 848726
Email: info@chandospublishing.com
www.chandospublishing.com

Chandos Publishing is an imprint of Woodhead Publishing Limited

Woodhead Publishing Limited
80 High Street
Sawston, Cambridge
CB22 3HJ, UK
www.woodheadpublishing.com
Tel: +44 (0) 1223 499140
Fax: +44 (0) 1223 832819

First published in 2011

ISBN:
978 1 84334 619 7

© S. Jelušić and I. Stričević

British Library Cataloguing-in-Publication Data.
A catalogue record for this book is available from the British Library.

Typeset by RefineCatch Limited, Bungay, Suffolk
Printed in the UK and USA.

Contents

Figures and tables

Acknowledgements

We are grateful to librarians from libraries of all kinds and all LIS students, our librarians to be, for it was their need for knowledge on the subject of library publishing that gave us the motivation to write this book. We are also most grateful to our colleagues with whom we have been discussing the need to devote attention to this segment of librarianship. We owe the deepest debt of gratitude to our families, who gave us their support while we worked on this book.

Special thanks go to Mirta Matošić, the manager of the University of Zadar library, who proofread the segments of the text written in English and translated the ones written in Croatian. Her comments and suggestions for additional explanations were especially valuable as she read the text from the standpoint of a librarian with an interest in publishing.

About the authors

Dr. Srećko Jelušić is currently vice rector in charge of international relations, publishing and library at the University of Zadar. He is associate professor teaching courses in research methods, information society, and information policy and technological change. Previously he also taught publishing and bookselling as well as 'sociology of a book'. He has been affiliated with universities for 10 years. His research interests are in reading habits and information needs in Croatia. Previously he managed the university library in Rijeka and worked as independent publisher. He has been editing books and magazines on culture, society and librarianship since 1976 and has translated several books in the field of information sciences. He has been a president of the Croatian Library Association and the Croatian Independent Publishers Association. His undergraduate studies were in comparative literature and sociology and he holds a PhD in library and information science.

Dr. Ivanka Stričević is assistant professor at the University of Zadar's Department of Library and Information Studies, teaching courses in information systems in education, literacies in the digital age, information services in educational institutions, library services for youth, and library users' rights and needs. In collaboration with Srećko Jelušić she continually researches information needs and reading habits in Croatia. Before teaching at the University of Zadar she worked in a public library as the manager of library services for youth. She was editor in chief of the Croatian Reading Association's journal for 10 years, co-authored and edited a number of books and wrote articles on pedagogy, early literacy and librarianship. Her undergraduate studies were in pedagogy and library and information science. She holds a Master's degree in pedagogy and a PhD in library and information science. She has been the chair of IFLA Literacy and Reading Section since 2007.

The authors can be contacted via the publisher.

Introduction

Abstract: The book deals with libraries as publishers in a variety of fields. It is meant for librarians and other information science professionals who are already involved, or will be, in the publishing process. It guides through the history of publishing, contemporary publishing, management of the publishing process and the role of various types of libraries in publishing.

Key words: library publishing, publishing management, publishing process

The aim of the book

Are you a librarian in a public, special, school, academic or national library? Perhaps you are a student who plans to work in one of these kinds of libraries, or a publisher who has an opportunity to cooperate with libraries and librarians on a publishing project. If any of these is true, then this book is for you. We wrote it to talk about publishing, and not just publishing in general, but publishing in and by libraries. So, this book is also about libraries and librarians, as without their efforts there would be no libraries or library publishing. Its aim is to professionalise the role of libraries in publishing and to teach the reader how to publish professionally. In essence, this book is intended for staff at managerial levels within libraries and teaching institutions. It will provide librarians with the know-how essential for successful accomplishment of publishing projects. It is also intended for library and information science students at graduate and postgraduate levels as a learning tool they can use to find out why publishing is a library function and how to approach it so the end result is a publication (print or electronic) that is valuable to their current and future users. The book can also be used in various publishing workshops for professionals, and all others who participate in the publishing process.

By 'publishing' we mean the process of production and dissemination of publications in print or electronic form. 'Publisher' is a person or a company engaged in publishing. To explain what a publication is, we take Borgman's definition (Borgman, 2007: 48), which states that 'publication occurs when a document is "made public" with an intention that it be read'. Therefore, we are talking about a process and about a product as a result of the process.

Publishing? Isn't publishing a publisher's job, and why should librarians learn about it?

Libraries have always been publishers – they issue a variety of publications, such as library catalogues, bibliographies, monographs, scientific papers, exhibition catalogues, periodicals and library operation reports. Libraries publish in print and electronic format. They create, edit, design and distribute the work, which they in turn use to communicate with their readers. We believe that in many libraries there is a lack of awareness about what percentage of library activities are related to library publishing. Creating and using library websites are making this even more apparent today. With the widespread use of the Internet, libraries' web pages are real publishing projects. But in many cases libraries lack the basic publishing principles in print as well as in digital publishing environments.

This book is intended as a guide that will enable librarians to take on successful publishing projects, help them avoid professional mistakes that may be damaging to the library's public image and possible cause of financial loss, equip managers with the skills for supervising the core publishing process and provide practical solutions to real-life work challenges. This does not mean that all libraries should take on the role of a publisher, but librarians are expected to be familiar with the basics of publishing in order to be able to organise a publishing process within their library and to know how to outsource parts of it. Following the set procedures can save time and money, and what is even more important, it ensures delivery of the desired publication on time and with envisioned content.

Background

Where do books come from? Is buying a book the same as going to any store and purchasing a desired product? What kind of a 'book' is a library's web page? How is it created? What are the ties between publishers and libraries? Is there a theory of library publishing? What about the questions of the future of print and of libraries? For those of us who work in the library and information field, times are indeed interesting. Due to rapid changes in this field, a great number of questions are raised daily. On the other hand, librarians and publishers have to keep their libraries steadily running and services improving as the users are ever more demanding. The convergence caused by the development of digital and virtual worlds is providing these two professions with immense opportunities as well as responsibilities. These responsibilities are complex and have influence on the future of humanity. Librarians and publishers have a say in creating our future as they have the ability to strongly affect the world of our ideas – we are what we think! Furthermore, users are no longer passive recipients of service; they are also active creators. Nevertheless, in a way, readers have always had an influence on publishing production because acceptance or rejection of printed works was a message to authors and publishers. Literary criticism and scientific reviewing are also forms of feedback from a reader to a publisher. In fact, aside from messengers in the Greek and Roman times, there has never been a way to react instantly to what was said to the audience. This postponed response we considered (or perhaps still consider) an advantage of print. And really, it still might be a good idea to think something over and then react. Interactive library websites do it differently; they enable users to instantly make comments and additions to the published data and photographs.

The complexity of the relationship between publishers and libraries arises from the simple fact that whatever enters a library collection is a publishing product, and nowadays every library product is a publication because it is publicly accessible. Here again users are an important driving force. Librarians have accepted it: libraries are for users. Donald Urquhart, a British librarian, was the first to state this clearly in his principles (Urquhart, 1981). Publishers must publish for readers. This means at least two things: librarians and publishers must know their readers well so that the published materials will respond to their needs and interests. Also, they have to consider how the published materials will reach the intended audience.

The authors of this book are of the opinion that the relationship between librarians and publishers should be closer than it is today, and that the digital environment creates new opportunities for cooperation, not for its own sake, but for the benefit of users. If librarians understand the basic publishing principles, their products will be better suited to their patrons – readers. If publishers understand the user-oriented philosophy of librarianship, their products will have a larger market. For this reason this book is intended for librarians who want to understand publishing and intend to be publishers themselves. 'Library publishing is the new hot topic,' stress Bankier and Smith (2008: 3), and they support this with examples of reports published in the past few years that show libraries' emerging role as publishers.

In the report *Research Library Publishing Services* conducted by the Association of Research Libraries (ARL), Hahn (2008) gives the results of analyses focused on libraries' production of journals and monographs in print or electronic or both forms. Out of 80 responding libraries, 44 per cent were delivering publishing services and 21 per cent were planning to do that. They mostly publish journals (88 per cent of respondents), conference papers and proceedings (71 per cent) and monographs (71 per cent). It is interesting that publishing services in those libraries are not treated as isolated units (as university press units might be) but as a part of other services, such as, for example, digital repository. The author points out that 'there is an emerging consensus that some sort of basic publishing services will become a core service for research libraries' (Hahn, 2008: 27). Librarians in the libraries with publishing services have a certain advantage over publishers: they are more familiar with the needs of the readers as they interact with them daily. Librarians have their fingers on the pulse of readers' needs, they can identify the issues that perhaps other publishing systems cannot recognise, they have the infrastructure – technology, staff expertise and partner relationship, they are able to reallocate existing resources, etc.

Moreover, many librarians are also authors. They are surrounded by a lot of reading materials and resources that they can use as inspiration for creating either professional publications or literary work. Some of that work is published by libraries. The book *Writing and Publishing: The librarian's handbook* (Smallwood, 2010) collects 47 accounts by librarians who write about their experiences in various roles of the publishing process, such as authoring different types of work, reviewing or editing.

All of this points to the need for librarians to be familiar with the publishing process as they can easily find themselves in the role of authors of a manuscript, facilitators of a publishing process, editors or other experts in the publication production, or all of the above.

Organisation of the book

This book is organised in nine chapters. After the introduction, an overview of the history of publishing – from scrolls to electronic publications – is given in Chapter 2. Our intention is to give a brief historic review because today's publishing leans on the historic forms, merges them with new ones and reveals new ways of publishing. Chapter 3 concentrates on many different aspects of the close relations between publishing, libraries and technology in order to explain the influence technology has on library publishing. Special attention is given to the technological development brought about by the introduction of computers into publishing and libraries. This development caused a gradual rise in library publishing activities as a consequence of the increased presence of new technologies that enabled librarians to master the knowledge and skills needed in the e-environment. This made libraries better equipped to fulfil their missions regarding more effective service to their users. Also explained are the reasons for e-transition in publishing. E-transition changes publications as well, so its influence to the convergence of media is explained. This convergence has provoked an e-shift in library services, including stronger publishing activities. In today's networked society, collaboration is not only an opportunity but a necessity. Partners contribute expertise, funding or whatever else might be their strength, while the gains are mutual.

In Chapter 4 the publishing fields are described, the term 'publishing capital' is explained and library publishing is placed between trade and non-commercial publishing. Libraries never publish for commercial purposes, though this does not mean that they cannot make a profit and invest it into new projects. The comparison of publishing capital between publishers and libraries shows that libraries have strong publishing capital, which explains their great potential in publishing projects. One of the strongest aspects of libraries' publishing capital is the librarians who are experts in numerous areas. Their expertise depends on their type of library. The fact is that libraries have always published, and today still, the variety of publications produced by libraries require that a librarian be well versed in publishing. First and foremost that means being familiar with the publishing process, its phases and dynamics. For this reason, Chapter 5 explains the steps of the publishing process. It describes the production of a professionally edited publication in accordance with a library's mission statement. Included are the main elements of a publishing plan: the timetable and the financial plan as prerequisites for publishing on time and within budget. This chapter is written in such a way that the steps described can be applied to both print and electronic publishing. An overview of the professions involved in publishing production follows in Chapter 6. The experts' contributions result in added value, which is an outcome of a publishing venture. Emphasis is placed equally on the descriptions of each profession as well as on their interdepencence. Each profession is described separately but it is clear that individual tasks can be combined and that one person can do more than one similar job, e.g. graphic editing and design, or language editing and proofreading. Finally, we explain the professional and social role of the statement of responsibility from the viewpoint of an author, a publisher and a reader.

Not all libraries are the same as they do not all publish the same kinds of books, so the publishing tasks are different in each library. For these reasons, in Chapter 7 we start with the basic distinction between national, university and research, special, school and public libraries and then we explain what kind of a publication is likely to be produced in each of these kinds of library. Here we also describe characteristics of an infrastructural phenomenon – the digital library, which is a publishing venture in itself. The emphasis is on research and university libraries because they have been going through a radical change during recent decades. In these libraries publishing used to be a marginal activity, whereas now publishing activities are some of the more important ones, especially in the digital environment. Repositories of scientific and educational papers open up new frontiers for these libraries, as through them libraries can better fulfil their primary missions. Librarians also publish outside of their libraries, sometimes through various international, regional and national library associations or associations of specific types of libraries. Chapter 8 explains the basis of co-publishing, the formal regulation of relations between co-publishing partners, some advantages (and possible disadvantages) of co-publishing and the motivation for co-publishing with the aim of bridging the digital divide. Libraries often co-publish. They enter into co-publishing relations on their own initiative, usually in order to facilitate the accomplishment of a publishing process, or through the initiative from a different publisher wishing to join forces with the libraries' publishing capital and with a goal of reaching synergy and producing an excellent final product that will also reach the public.

In Chapter 9 we highlight major points made throughout the book and we conclude that publishing is one of the library services that is becoming increasingly important. This means that librarians and those who will become librarians should be familiar with some elements of publishing in order to strengthen the role of libraries as publishers.

Finally, there are two appendices. The aim of the first is to advise libraries on how to assess their past publishing activities and use them as a basis for development of the strategic plan. Appendix 2 gives the basic principles to be followed in order to improve publishing activities in the future, so that they result in strengthening libraries' position in the society.

While writing this book we chose to describe principles and processes of library publishing in general, and we only emphasise specific print or electronic publishing requirements when needed. Nowadays it is not possible to seriously discuss publishing without paying attention to electronic publishing. Electronic publishing offers tremendous opportunities for libraries in all aspects of publishing, such as searching for, preparation of and writing the manuscript, as well as processing, designing, producing and distributing the publication to its end users. New technologies also have an effect on the process of making a print publication, as it allows for better, faster and more effective communication of all involved in the publication production chain all the way to the reader. The proof of this is in the process of making this book, where the authors collaborated on it even though they live 300 kilometres away from each other, and the publisher is five times as far away.

2

Brief overview of the history of publishing

Abstract: The chapter gives an overview of the historical evolution of publishing media in chronological sequence. Significant geographical locations and historical individuals are mentioned. An overview of interaction between the technological development of the carrier of information and content presentation is given, from clay tablets and scrolls to the formats used in print and electronic technology. The role of libraries and librarians in relation to publishers and publishing is discussed in respect to the major media forms.

Key words: publishing history, clay tablets, scrolls, codices, printed books

Clay tablets

We are all familiar with the following crucial moments in human history: the clay tablets, the parchment writings, the manuscripts, the progress from the scroll to the codex and what it meant for the readers and for the development of the human mind. We want to draw attention to their development, in which librarians and scribes played a very important role. Today we must be aware of these turning points in history and the complexity of relations between print, publishing and librarianship with their discoveries and inventions. Throughout the history of development of Western culture and science, the accumulation of knowledge has always been essential.

The Sumerian clay tablet – with pictorial writing from the end of the fourth century BC – is the oldest scripture discovered to this day and the city of Nippur, where it was discovered, had a district with scriptoriums (Kramer, 1981). After the Sumerians, the Babylonians continued to write on clay tablets and to store them in libraries in Mesopotamia. However, the most significant clay tablet library was that of the Assyrian king Asurbanipal (seventh century BC). In his library an army of scribes copied each text, sometimes several times over.

Scrolls and codices

The most common writing material in Egypt was papyrus, a material already in use at the beginning of the third millennium BC. Papyrus was exported from Egypt to other parts of the world, from the eleventh century, to Phoenicians and Syrians, and later to Greeks and Romans. It was the most common writing material until parchment and paper replaced it. Egyptian books had a scroll shape, a form that continued to later times, especially in Greece and Rome (Černy, 1952). Before the invention of paper in China, strips of bamboo, bones, wooden tablets, stone and later silk were used as writing material. These surfaces were unsuitable and difficult to handle so there were many reasons to invent a better material for writing. Historians believe that paper was invented in China in the first century BC (Blum, 1934).

In Greece, especially during the fourth century BC, the scroll book became the primary mode of communication, and this marked the definitive shift from oral to written culture. The first professional scribes and bookstores in

Athens appeared as early as the fifth century BC but the distribution of these books was modest and difficult (Kenyon, 1951). Before the golden age of the Alexandria library in the third century BC, Rhodes, Antioch, Pergamum and especially Alexandria become important centres of book production and trade. Aside from the affluent individuals, the biggest book buyers were libraries. Decentralisation of the Hellenistic world and its culture contributed to the final affirmation of the written word.

When we are talking about this time period, the Etruscan civilisation must not go unmentioned. The so-called Zagreb mummy was wrapped in a sort of a codex, which is the only known cloth 'book' preserved from this period. This 13.5-meter-long codex is the longest Etruscan text known to this day (Dumezil, 1977).

Ancient Rome continued the well-established Greek tradition of book production in the form of the scroll up to the second century AD. A very important change in book form occurs in the period from the second to the fourth century AD. Parchment is increasingly taking the place of papyrus, and instead of a scroll, books are more often taking the shape of a codex. This shift outlived the ancient world and dominated book production until Gutenberg invented the printing press. The domination of parchment over papyrus also had a deeper social meaning. It coincides with the domination of Christianity over pagan beliefs. Christians and Jews regarded a sacred text as an object that had to be preserved and therefore to be written on a surface that was more durable than papyrus. Also, papyrus was not as suited for illustrations as was parchment. This is a very important moment in the history of the book. Papyrus supported only water colours, which would crack and fall off while bending the scroll. Illustrations on parchment, on the other hand, were durable. Besides fixed colours, the codex had the advantage of the rectangular shape

13

of pages, which allowed the illustrator to design a better layout of the text and illustrations. In spite of all of these advantages, the scroll remained and was treasured until the sixth century AD. With regard to access to and quality of information, the time period we are describing here played an important role in the transmitting of information, as the contents from the scrolls were massively copied to the codex format. This was of tremendous importance for the preservation of old texts that would otherwise disappear. Books made at the end of the ancient era were often illustrated and bound. With the conquest of Christianity over paganism, parchment won out over papyrus.

Highlights from the history of publishing – from papyrus to Gutenberg

Eleventh century BC – the age of papyrus

The most common writing material in Egypt was the papyrus, a material already in use at the beginning of the third millennium BC. Papyrus was exported from Egypt to other parts of the world, from the eleventh century to the Phoenicians and Syrians, and later to the Greeks and Romans. It was the most common writing material until parchment and paper replaced it. The Egyptian book always had a scroll shape.

Seventh century BC – the age of clay tablets

The most significant clay tablet library was that of the Assyrian king Asurbanipal. An army of scribes copied each text sometimes several times over.

Fifth century BC – the age of Greek bookstores

The first professional scribes and bookstores in Athens appeared as early as the fifth century BC, but the distribution of these books was modest and difficult.

(Cont'd)

Fourth century BC – the age of pictorial writing

The Sumerian clay tablet with pictorial writing from the end of the fourth century BC is the oldest scripture discovered to this day. The city of Nippur had a district of scriptoriums. After the Sumerians, the Babylonians continued to write on clay tablets and to store them in libraries in Mesopotamia.

Third century BC – the age of Alexandria

The golden age of the Alexandrian library, the biggest and richest library of the ancient world, was also the important centre of book production and trade. Apart from rich individuals, the biggest book buyers were libraries. The decentralisation of the Hellenistic world and its culture brought about the affirmation of the written word.

First century BC – the invention of paper in China

Historians think that paper was invented in China in the first century BC. Before the invention of paper, strips of bamboo, bones, wooden tablets, stone and later silk were used as writing material. These surfaces were unsuitable and difficult to handle so there were many reasons to invent a better material for writing.

Second to fourth century – the age of the scroll

Ancient Rome continued the well-established Greek tradition of book production in the form of the scroll up to the second century. A very important transformation for books occured from the second to the fourth century. Parchment increasingly took the place of papyrus, and instead of a scroll, books were more often taking the shape of a codex. This shift outlived the ancient world and dominated book production until Gutenberg's time.

Sixth to fifteenth century – the age of codex

The contents from the scrolls were massively copied to the codex format. The skills to illustrate and bind were

(Cont'd)

abundantly used at the end of ancient times. With the conquest of Christianity over paganism, parchment won out over papyrus.

Fifteenth century – the invention of print with movable type

Johann Gutenberg invented the print with movable type. Gutenberg's invention enabled printers to use movable type instead of a plate, which could be used for one book only, while movable type could be used to print many books.

Print

The importance of print is evident to all librarians. The study of the history of print is a part of librarians' education, and research on books is conducted in many countries. Such studies include the history of print and printers and it seems that this research area is limitless. A number of times in recent book history, the end of print has been predicted. The reason for this was the advent of computers. Publishers and librarians equally were exposed to theories about libraries without walls and paperless offices. Theories about the end of print were confronted with theories of permanence. However, all of this is happening in an age of integration, when each new technology is integrated into the old. The same happens with electronic publishing and its integration into print publishing, the result of which is that today we not only witness hybrid libraries but also hybrid publications.

So, what should librarians get out of this? Are the librarians who talk of the renaissance of libraries in the right or in the wrong? New libraries of all kinds are being built, especially public and university libraries. New ways of access to unique sources are continually being invented. In this jungle on the web, as Saracevic (2000) calls it, libraries are gaining importance as institutions because in the flood of information, the information can lose its meaning. Libraries are here to preserve important content. In hyper-production of printed and electronic books, a library is a guarantee of quality. If they join forces with publishers, the production of quality can be even stronger. This goes for historic and church libraries as well. Libraries are changing while maintaining their essence. The printed book is the fundamental part of this essence. The continuity of libraries and of printed material as the essence of libraries is vital proof that these two phenomena are the basis of human culture, not only Western but also globally. Just imagine how rich Johann Gutenberg would have been had he, or anyone else who invented moveable print, had the means to protect this patent with a copyright. We don't know if anyone ever tried to calculate his hypothetical profit, but it surely would have generated a small fortune.

So, from both historical and contemporary points of view, the coexistence of printed and electronic text will continue with endless variations of overlapping and dominance. With time the enthusiasm for digitisation will diminish to more justifiable intensity. We are still witnessing great excitement and faith in digitisation as well as lack of research on its use and effectiveness. In many countries it is much easier to get funding for digitisation than for research on its effects. We are not ignoring the fact that a new generation of users is growing up. The digital-born generation has new reading habits and it seems that they will keep their digital habits for life. What their attitude towards print will be will probably primarily depend on the reading habits they develop (or not) in early childhood, as well as on the format they been accustomed to in early childhood. However, when observing their views about print, it should be taken into account that book-like electronic reading is rapidly growing in use and commercial benefit (Renear and Salo, 2003) followed by a variety of devices, software and distribution systems. These factors open up new possibilities for publishing in general.

3

Technology-driven publishing and libraries

Abstract: This chapter explains the influence of the development of technology on media, libraries and publishing. Historical and contemporary examples of the interconnection between technology and publishing are given, starting from early stages to contemporary developments. Attention is given to new developments in publishing in the electronic environment, with emphasis on libraries as publishers, and on e-transition and its influence on the convergence of media. Advantages of electronic publishing are described, especially in regard to academic libraries as e-publishers.

Key words: technology-driven publishing, libraries and e-publishing, e-transition, media convergence, publishing services

Publishing and technology

Publishing is technology-driven. Librarians are well aware of how technology can affect the development of a profession. This is the case for society as a whole and it is especially important for information professions. Since publishing and librarianship are both information professions, the link between their development and technology is a dialectic one. As we will not explore the theoretical side of dialectics here, we want to stress how important it is to channel the development of technology according to the needs of our users. It is important for librarians to be aware of the fact that technology is not socially neutral (Hofkirchner, 2007).

Technology is designed to produce certain outcomes. But due to its ambiguous nature, technology can produce unforeseen outcomes. This is why the choice of technology is very important, and librarians have to be aware that their choice will have wide social consequences.

It has never been possible to separate publishing from technology. Technology was needed to prepare the surface on which to write, even in the past; for example, stone graffiti was also produced using technology, although in a simple form. It has remained so until today. However, the degree of closeness of the publisher as a person to technology changed through time. Maybe the 'officina' of Aldus Manutius (1450–1515) was a real publishing heaven – set in flourishing Venice, the queen of the world and the Mediterranean, as well as the market for Manutius's books. The structure of the publishing house, consisting of a printing press, a bindery, a bookshop and a room at the top of the house to accommodate the author, was a complete publishing universe. After Manutius, the development of publishing in its contemporary form started. However, the basic principles, established only several decades after Johann Gutenberg's (c.1398–1468) invention of moveable letters, remain applicable to this day. The idea behind Manutius's actions was to spread knowledge. He was convinced that he could better serve society by taking on printing than by continuing to teach. Following this principle, he printed books that could be carried around. Nothing unusual for us today, but then it was revolutionary. Before the invention of the octavo book format, books could not be carried around because they were too large and heavy. The change in format was a big step forward in book production. In the sixteenth century, Europe was still far from mass literacy, but at least the people who could read – and this was a new class – could now carry their books around. This is why Gutenberg and Manutius remain the two beacons of early printing and publishing. And, as far as technology was concerned, printing and publishing were not separate activities. A printer was a publisher. Did we not witness the same situation at the advent of electronic publishing? Those who were computer-savvy at once became publishers. Before that, Marshall McLuhan had predicted mass publishing by means of the photocopying machine, which could turn every author into a publisher (McLuhan et al., 1967). Later on McLuhan changed his mind, becoming aware of publishing as a process that involves not only the author but also other professionals.

Although ambiguous, technology is seductive. Ambiguity of technology is maybe best compared to the examples of medical drugs and nuclear energy. Both, if used properly, are helpful, but used in an inappropriate way can cause harm or disaster. There are examples of experts in various fields who became printers because they were enchanted by technology. Although printing is repetitive work, whenever a new title is printed the publisher is excited. Being aware of the fact that what is being printed will reach many readers gives publishers a great sense of worth. With electronic publishing the publisher is left without this palpable feeling. The lack of tangible sensation of handling a bound book can be rationally compensated by the awareness of speed and instant worldwide distribution of the published content. However, today publishing and printing are separate. There are very few examples of publishers who also own printing houses and print books in-house. Even in countries with small print runs due to their small language distribution, the printing industry is separate from publishing. Publishers are turning to their main responsibilities – acquisition and editing of manuscripts. They outsource most of the work that once was done within the publishing house: design and layout, printing, binding and distribution. This means that publishers nowadays do not need advanced technology. Design and layout studio equipment, powerful scanners, photo cameras and advanced computers are not necessary as most publishers outsource this kind of work, often to the Middle East or Asia. The same is done with printing, but mainly for high-volume print runs.

POD stands for 'print on demand' or 'publish on demand'. POD has opened a whole new set of possibilities for publishers. Although limiting as far as quality is concerned and not adequate for more demanding printing jobs, POD has enabled (especially scholarly) publishers to have a limitless backlist. This method is especially suited for textbooks. There are many academic titles that are not graphically demanding and can be produced with POD technology. POD is a good example of technological advancement in publishing, and it has also resulted in a new business model. For certain types of publication, this means they may never go out of print.

The e-transition in publishing

Libraries and publishers have always worked together as they share the audience for which they both provide books, each in their own way. This joint effort gets a new dimension in the transition process brought about by the emergence of electronic publishing and electronic publications, but also the process of transition itself gets a new, more complex dimension. This complexity of the transition from print to electronic arises from the fact that two different institutions, publishers and libraries, join forces in creating a new product based on new technological infrastructure and environment.

To face and solve this complexity, new editing and new business models are needed. Johnson and Luther argue:

> While it shares the widely held assumption that we are headed to a world in which purely electronic journals are the norm, this research was not designed to advance an agenda for or against various approaches to e-only publishing of journals. Rather it seeks to better understand the dynamics of the transition process. Publishers and librarians were consulted equally in recognition that these changes pose significant issues of coordination. A synthetic analysis of the situation is sorely needed. Neither publishers nor librarians independently control the process. The need to somehow coordinate their activities greatly increases the complexity of the transition. (Johnson and Luther, 2007: v)

When we set out to write this chapter, we were initially going to deal with three separate topics: print publications, electronic publications and hybrid publications. Later in the process we changed our minds as we realised this division would have been valid in the initial developmental stages of electronic publications, but no longer today. For that reason we decided that the aim of this chapter is to explain the ways in which technological changes have influenced the emergence of new formats and supported publishing activities in libraries, and why ICT (information and communication technology) was a significantly greater incentive for such activity than the earlier publishing technologies that different media used. We must recall development paths of some media other than paper in order to observe the speed of the transitions. These transitions often go unnoticed. Who remembers floppy disks and how many Kb they stored? More people will remember a 3.5-inch disk because it was used for software distribution before CDs became widely used. These technological changes happened fast and we no longer use the floppy or 3.5-inch disk.

Who remembers view cameras? Many people have never seen the glass negatives that were still in use at the beginning of the twentieth century. They were the size of a postcard and they allowed the reproduction of large format photographs with excellent sharpness and tone. Most family photos up to the 1960s were black and white. Photographs and diapositives in colour appeared later. Although Vannevar Bush in 1945 predicted the possibility of instantaneously seeing the photographed image, it was not until several decades later that digital photography was invented.

Who remembers 78 rpm Bakelite records and steel needles affixed to a speaker that emitted a shrill sound? Those who listened to music on the early phonograms will remember how often the handle needed to be turned to wind it up in order for the sound to be even and the music well reproduced. Who remembers jukeboxes and singles? When the vinyl revolution conquered the world, wind-up phonograms became history. We hadn't quite forgotten them when CDs appeared on the scene.

What to do with an old videocassette? They used to be the cutting-edge technology in the time when 8mm black-and-white movies amused families at home, and their cousins – 16 and 32mm films – entertained cinema audiences. Radio with a turntable (also called a *cabinet*) used to be a massive, freestanding, impressive piece of furniture. Every respectable family had to have one. Whoever peeked into the mechanism of these machines would have seen a multitude of vacuum tubes of all sizes. Battery-operated, portable transistor radios had still not been invented at that time.

Who remembers the first black and white television sets and the shows that opened with images of a raising curtain such as in a theatre?

Did we skip something? Magnetic tape players, telephones, voice recorders, all these content-storing or transmitting devices could tell long stories of transformation. So, faster or slower technological changes have been with us for a long time, but what is especially interesting to us is that these changes always affected libraries. Naturally, not all libraries were equally affected. However, it makes a big difference for a library whether a photograph is on paper or digital. The situation is similar for the other media we mentioned. What is significant for librarians today is that with the development of technology, it has become possible to store all content on one single medium – a computer disc. CDs can be used for storing various types of records, and with the appropriate technology these records can be accessed. Content that once was stored on various media such as paper, glass, celluloid, Bakelite, vinyl and magnetic tape is now kept on small plastic discs. And not only does the CD (or the Internet) carry and/or reproduce the content, but the content can also be successfully combined and mutually complemented. Publication is no longer linear and it cannot be read linearly. Let us consider a web manual with links to various web pages, expanding its content through other sources on the net, through web movies, audio recordings, knowledge tests for feedback purposes, or 3D virtual walks. We can also consider a printed book that is only fully utilised if the included CD-ROM with, for example, speech exercises or videos is used. Such publications are hybrid media as they are a fusion of two or more formats. They converge as multiple products coming together to form one product with the advantages of all of them.

Possibilities for interconnecting content are limitless and the electronic environment not only changes formats but also content as it gives it more depth and breadth. Producing such publications involves not only the usual publishing experts but also a wide spectrum of other professionals, such as video producers and information specialists who can find and interlink the sources on the web. Technological advancement brought libraries into an entirely new dimension. It brought new possibilities, but along with it many dilemmas and problems. Computer catalogues, library information systems, e-publishing, collection digitalisation, and plenty other possibilities opened up for libraries with the emergence of ICT. On the other side of the coin were considerations of acquisition ratios of printed over electronic materials, decisions on joining library consortia, digitalisation priorities and so forth. There were issues about how to decide whether to acquire or publish electronic or print versions of a publication, how durable the digital medium would be, whether digitalisation is a measure of preservation, what will be the cost of document reformatting in the future, how to manage staff who work in new technologies, what employee profiles to hire, and finally the issue of coordination with the publishers as it is not possible for just one side without the other to have the control over the transition process from print to electronic.

Everything that pertains to libraries has a bearing on its publishing activity – new opportunities but also new problems and dilemmas.

As the benefits of e-publishing were appreciated, potential difficulties were recognised. The most prominent potential difficulty that was identified was establishing the authenticity of published work. With the advent of electronic publication came awareness of the fact that the electronic medium is very susceptible to abuse. These fears were partially based on the experiences with illegal photocopying. This was another case of a new technology proving to be helpful as much as harmful. People used illegal photocopying in place of, for example, subscribing to a journal or getting a library membership. Computers offered far greater possibilities than copy machines but even greater opportunities for pirating someone else's work.

The situation was complicated further by issues of interoperability and standardisation due to the variety of hardware and software. These problems were eventually solved, but in the beginning the situation was so complex that subscribers of the first electronic journals needed specific hardware and software in order to view journals they subscribed to. In an exaggerated scenario, had the issue of interoperability and standardisation not been solved, a library would have required separate hardware and software for each journal subscription. Imagine such a scenario for a library that subscribes to over 1,000 journals.

As we see throughout this book and other literature, libraries have always published a variety of documents. Using available technology is not a foreign concept to a librarian because book-binding and printing were often part of library operations. However, sometimes libraries were cautious when adopting new technologies and this was the case with computer technologies. However, it was soon realised that computers were ideal for library operations. Libraries became competitors to some companies that took over tasks traditionally done by libraries, such as creating databases, scholarly journal abstracts or indexing. It is necessary for libraries to redefine their social role, which today is much wider than it was before ICT. From a marginal position in ICT, libraries became its teachers, but all in accordance with the needs of their patrons. Libraries publish electronically those publications that are consistent with their mission, and they teach information literacy to all users so that they can utilise electronic publishing.

But what does it all have to do with libraries and publishing? What if libraries still were to deal with Bakelite or vinyl records, a glass negative, or a magnetic tape? Amazing new opportunities open up for libraries. Their collections can be more accessible than ever before. And when we take a closer look at the technological advancements of machines we use or see in our daily life, we notice that they all have common traits: technology replaces the human work (think of how much craft was needed to make a photograph, from handling the camera, to film development, to printing – all these tasks are taken over by technology nowadays); technology expedites all described processes. Previously unthinkable speed caused the need for it to be introduced as a criterion for all human actions. Usage of technology becomes individualised and on a mass scale. Instead of a whole family going to a photographer's once a year for a family photo, each family member has their own digital photo or video camera. These trends affect all aspects of human life, thus leading to radical changes in libraries. If we consider the listed examples and look back in time, we can see how much of human work in libraries was replaced by technology – from the basic tasks of getting books from the stacks, creating databases and union catalogues to harvesting electronic publications. Searching online catalogues takes a fraction of a second while searching a card catalogue can take hours, sometimes days of a librarian's time. Access to library collections has always been a matter of individual choice, but patrons accessed the collections through card catalogues that existed in single copy and that could be used by a limited number of patrons at the same time. Searching through the 'A' drawer in the card catalogue could only be done by one patron or librarian at a time. Nowadays, the number of simultaneous users of a library catalogue is virtually limitless.

For example, what is happening with a publishing product of a national library – a national bibliography? It is a responsibility of the national library to publish the national bibliography. The effort is made to decrease expenses and increase the possibility of simultaneous access. Those two criteria are the main benefits of electronic publishing. Let us consider an example from the National Library of Germany. Svensson and Jahns (2010) describe the changes in the German National Bibliography format. Until 2009 it was published as a print journal, then later as a CD-ROM. To lower the cost of production and distribution, since 2010 the bibliography is published as an online journal. However, it is not only the format that changed from print to electronic and online, but also the value added service that enables web 2.0 with the purpose '. . . to introduce alerting services based on the user's search criteria offering different access methods such as RSS feeds, integration with e.g. Zotero, or export of the bibliographic data as a CSV or PDF file' (Svensson and Jahns, 2010: 1). The patrons get the bibliographic data but also the opportunity to express and satisfy their specific needs – to customise the publication to their own desires.

If these technological trends are put in context with earlier described trends in journal subscription price increases, it becomes apparent that this combination of factors influenced one more significant change: the libraries, especially the research ones, are turning towards publishing and in such a way as to utilise every opportunity electronic publishing offers.

Some authors emphasise that due to the way books are made, each book is actually an e-book, especially with the advent of print on demand (POD). Kovač states:

> The background of this similarity between the PoD book and music digital files is the very fact that with the exception of the paper on which it is printed, the book today is produced exclusively via digital technology

> and The book: this charming old lady is being marketed in a similar way to digital music files. We might say that according to its marketing and production properties, a *de facto* digitally printed book is essentially an e-book, albeit printed and stored on an 'analogue' platform. (Kovač, 2008: 13)

However, does the opposite hold true in a sense that thanks to POD each electronic book can be available in print format? There are indeed many limitations in this case, especially when it comes to hybrid publications. By printing the earlier mentioned manual with links to audio and video recordings, its meaning would be lost. We can say that a 'step backward' (from electronic to print) is not possible for many kinds of electronic publications, while a 'step forward' (from print to electronic) definitely opens greater possibilities for enriching the content of a publication, improves accessibility and adjusts better to the needs of an individual customer – a reader.

E-publishing and libraries

Compared with the history of publishing in general, e-publishing has a short history, no longer than four decades. Naturally, the advent of the Internet and digital technologies changes the content and access to documents. All of that opens new opportunities for the publishing industry. Electronics and libraries have a history of a mutual relationship, with its ups and downs. It seems that only in recent years librarians and computer specialists started to collaborate on an equal footing. In some countries such collaboration started as early as the 1960s and in other countries some time later. The collaboration was fruitful in environments where computer specialists and librarians were in equal positions, and it was devastating where one or the other gained the dominant position. We are all too familiar with the jokes inspired by librarians' conservatism. The prejudice of conservative librarians was perhaps the most evident during joint projects with computer specialists. It is true that many librarians were not eager to accept new technologies. This is possibly a consequence of centuries-long and established library services that were run without computers. Apprehension towards new technologies was to be expected as their introduction was to change libraries' organisational structure. Emergence of entirely new and until then unknown kinds of library professional brought about a new technological culture that was considered by some to be more valuable than the existing one. It is not surprising that it took several decades and a lot of uncertainty until it became apparent that libraries and computers would be a good match.

Publishing was quicker to accept new technologies. It, however, is primarily business oriented. Also, the expectations that publishing initially had of computers were more modest and revolved mainly around word processing. Only later were they used for creating databases for improved accessibility and distribution.

Today computers are the most basic tool in publishing as well as in libraries; therefore one can say with certainty that all libraries are equipped for publishing. Naturally, libraries have published before the computer era, but never before have they been so technologically equipped for the task. There is no doubt that being technologically equipped is one of the more significant incentives for the libraries to undertake publishing projects.

Today libraries no longer collaborate only with publishers but also with so-called aggregators. Aggregators collect e-books from various publishers and make them available to libraries, among others, in various formats. Vasileiou et al., in their overview of the e-book marketplace, argue that electronic books have 'a similar or arguably a more significant potential to impact on information behaviours, with important consequences for the future role and existence of libraries' (Vasileiou et al., 2009: 173). Does this mean that librarians have to understand the world of electronic publishing and change their services accordingly in order to survive in the business, or will electronic publishing undermine their role regardless of their efforts and competencies? In the context of library publishing we believe that the former scenario is the likely one. Information environment, writing, editing, design and distribution of documents change, but those who can adapt to and actively participate in the changes may be certain that the new technologies will not threaten their position in the 'services market'.

Many authors who deal with publishing issues nowadays analyse the advantages that electronic publishing may have over traditional publishing.[1] To emphasise a few:

- Automation of production shortens the time needed to publish a manuscript.
- Electronic publishing can reduce costs.
- Multiple types of production are possible.
- The product can be available and updated at any stage of production.
- Possibility of use goes beyond the basic text.
- Print on demand is an option, etc.

Kovacs agrees that aside from other advantages – such as simultaneous access by a limitless number of readers, ease of collection development in regards to space, preservation through duplication and archiving – electronic publishing has an additional advantage, namely the opportunity for libraries to become publishers (Kovacs, 1999). Libraries, and especially the academic ones, use this opportunity through publishing their own e-journals, e-newsletters and other materials. The author emphasises that the issue of how the emergence and presence of e-publications impact the people who read them is more important than '. . . what we will do with the machines, the storage media or the delivery mechanisms' (Kovacs, 1999: 9).

However, to take advantage of the potential that electronic publishing offers, a basic knowledge of the technology and possible formats is necessary. Although electronic publishing involves experts outside of the library profession, librarians should be familiar with the potential the new technologies offer to be able to choose the best way to publish their work and present it to the public.

Note

1. For example, see *Why Publishers Should Use XML* . . ., available from *http://www.dclab.com/stm_xml.asp* (accessed 15 July 2010).

4

An overview of publishing fields and publishing capital

Abstract: Each type of book is different and each publication belongs to a different publishing field. In this chapter we explain the elements by which a publishing field is defined. Special attention is given to the components of publishing capital: economic, human, symbolic and intellectual. We elaborate on the reasons as to why libraries as distinguished public institutions inherently possess certain kinds of publishing capital and which other kinds they have to develop in order to become equal partners in certain publishing areas.

Key words: publishing fields, publishing capital, trade publishing, non-commercial publishing

Let us start with a comparison. Consider two books: a children's picture book and an encyclopaedia. We will begin by comparing their formal and content characteristics. Formal characteristics include format, type of paper, typography, binding, print, etc. Content characteristics are the text and illustrations.

Suppose that typography (print) from the encyclopaedia is used as text in a children's picture book, or the other way around. Then suppose that the illustration of a horse or a cow from the picture book is used in the encyclopaedia, or the other way around. The readers would certainly be confused and such books would be useless. There are children's encyclopaedias where it is appropriate to use the above-mentioned combinations; however, those are special publications, adjusted to the readers' age.

There are a number of comparisons we could conduct; however, the ones above are sufficient to illustrate the point that each type of book serves its own purpose. The type of book a publisher chooses to publish depends on their publishing field. Roughly speaking, a field is a structured space of social positions whose properties are defined primarily by the relations between these positions and by the resources attached to them. We can conceptualise the publishing field as a space of positions occupied by different publishing organisations. The position of any particular publisher depends on the number of resources they possess. What kinds of resources do publishers possess (Thompson, 2005: 30)? Thompson found four key types of resources important for publishing firms: economic capital, human capital, symbolic capital and intellectual capital.

Let us see which of these resources libraries possess.

Economic capital

A library is a public institution, and it is financed and maintained by its founder. There are different degrees of independence between libraries and their founders; however, libraries always fulfil a mission that is in accordance with the mission of their founder. So, if libraries are working according to their plan, they can expect to be financed in order to accomplish their goal. If publishing becomes a part of a library's strategy and consequently a part of its plan, the economic capital – which is the most important and sometimes the most difficult to acquire for a trade publisher – will be provided. The public view of libraries is that of being stable and systematic institutions that do not engage in risky and unpredictable actions. A library will behave in the same fashion when publishing is concerned. The produced publication will be one of the things that contributes to fulfilment of the library's mission, and as such it will be planned in advance and the budget for its production will be secured. We could conclude that every library in fact has the economic capital needed for publishing but that publishing activities will be proportional to the economic power of a library.

Human capital

This is another strong point for libraries. Experts of various backgrounds work in libraries. This gives libraries the possibility to undertake publishing projects that rely on the knowledge of their librarians and on their collections. Over the past two or three decades, the whole library system, including training of librarians, has seen great changes in the curriculum. Library schools worldwide are very aware of the changes in the library environment and have adapted their curricula accordingly. Librarians and libraries as well as librarianship are highly connected and networked, nationally and internationally. ICT has given a new impulse to traditionally highly organised professional associations of librarians. Therefore, many factors contribute to the fact that libraries are staffed with highly educated and professional employees. While a trade publisher has to search the labour market for experts of such calibre, a library has them at home. Librarians interact with publications daily and directly and are also familiar with publishing. This is why human capital is one of libraries' strong features when it comes to publishing. Librarians inherently know a good publication when they see one.

Symbolic capital

On the priority list of public institutions, libraries rank very high. They have existed since books were first made and they have survived the digital revolution. Their number is increasing, their functions and services are growing and their social responsibilities are becoming more significant. A society with prominent libraries is regarded as a highly civilised and democratic society with high cultural values. Libraries are respected by members of society and public opinion is very sensitive to what is happening to the libraries in their communities. This is why national libraries are regarded as icons, as symbols of nations. Hence this symbolic capital – which a trade or other publisher has to build up for years, even decades, and which can be destroyed with one wrong publishing decision or investment – is in fact the essence of a library.

Intellectual capital

This concerns the publishing rights of a publisher. A library that decides to publish something will have to work hard to gradually build this sort of capital. As far as intellectual capital is concerned, a library does not have the same advantage over a publisher as it has in economic, human and symbolic capital. When compared with publishers, libraries have smaller intellectual publishing capital. One of the main goals of a publisher is to produce as many titles with as many years of publishing rights as possible. Libraries, on the other hand, do not publish as often, so they start accruing the intellectual publishing capital only after a longer period or more intensive publishing.

All four kinds of capital are necessary in order to publish. It is astonishing how much publishing capital, as defined by Thompson, libraries have. The central placement of libraries in Figure 4.1 is a result of their publishing activities that are intended for both the general and specialised market. This placement is based on the capital libraries have available and this is why they can decide to enter one market or the other, or to distribute their efforts evenly to both markets.

Various publications listed on the scheme could also be library publications, but here we might be more inclined to the right side of the scheme, especially if we consider partnering with university presses. On the other hand, public and school libraries might deliver publications that are listed on the left hand side of the scheme. So it all really depends on the library type and the library's mission.

Figure 4.1   Publishing for general and specialised markets

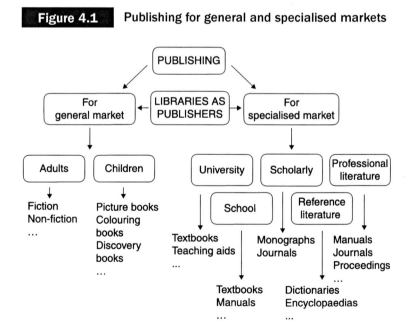

Being essentially non-profit organisations, based on their publishing capital libraries can decide to enter the publishing market and dedicate part of their activities to trade publishing. Libraries don't publish for profit but they can sell a part of their print run in order to get a return on investment, or, in the case of electronic publication, find another way to make a profit (such as pay per view). It is our belief that even in partnering with trade publishers libraries will continue to follow their mission to serve their community and their final decision about market and trade will rely on this.

5

Basics of the library publishing chain

Abstract: This chapter explains the basic business and professional steps necessary for making a strong publishing chain that will result in a quality publication. This is applicable to publishing in general, and to library publishing as well. The importance of consistent implementation of all elements of the publishing chain is emphasised and special attention is given to problems that publishers might encounter if an element is omitted. Basic reasons for library publishing are discussed, as well as decisions on what to publish, and whether to publish in print or electronic format. Fundamental elements of library publishing management are described: editorial team, planning, manuscript acquisition and contracting, production and distribution.

Key words: steps in the library publishing process, planning in library publishing, library publishing management

Where to start and how to manage the process

The starting point of the publishing process is to become familiar with the steps necessary for the process and product to be successful. The steps of the process go from the reasons for publishing and the choice of publication to communication with the readers once the publication process is completed.

Basic steps:

- identifying the need to publish
- getting a clear idea about the planned publication
- deciding on format (print or electronic, or both?)
- setting up an editorial board
- studying the audience
- creating a publishing plan; identifying human, material and financial resources and drawing up a timetable
- commissioning a manuscript or manuscripts (or writing it)
- selecting a manuscript
- talking to author/s and preparing contract/s
- hiring or assigning experts for reviewing process (if planned), then for language editing
- hiring or assigning experts to create a layout
- choosing a graphic designer
- approving the layout
- arranging for proofreading
- approving the print dummy
- sending materials to a printer, publishing electronically, or both
- strategising about marketing and creating a marketing plan
- distributing and delivering the publication
- recording feedback and considering it in a future publishing process.

These are the basic steps of a professional publishing process. Skipping one or more steps may cause difficulties that will be impossible or expensive to correct, or will even cause failure of the entire project. Who is to perform these steps and how it should be done is explained below and in Chapter 6.

Scenario 1: N.N. is a librarian in an academic library. He encounters students' information issues on a daily basis, especially with the first-year students who have poor information literacy skills. Students have highly developed computer literacy skills and they have no problems using computers and the Internet. They actually prefer the Internet as their source of information. However, their problem is their underdeveloped information searching strategies. They do not know how to use library catalogues and databases efficiently, they have trouble finding relevant information and once they find information they don't know how to evaluate. It is clear that the students need help improving their basic information literacy skills.

The library manager assigned librarian N.N. to design an online tutorial that will help students become familiar with research strategies and evaluation of information sources. The first step, 'Identify the need', is obvious as there is an evident need for an education tool. N.N. suggests creating an online tutorial because the students prefer using the Internet. There are other benefits to such a format as the tool can be used by many students simultaneously, the cost of making it is not too high, it can be updated and added to if needed and it allows for immediate feedback on success of the completion of the course, which will stimulate the students' learning. Hence, an online tutorial appears to be the best product solution.

N.N. rounds up the editorial board. He is familiar with the problem and the content of the future tutorial; however, he will include an e-learning expert on the board as N.N. isn't quite proficient with teaching/learning strategies. He will also include an information systems specialist who is familiar with issues such as customisation, scalability, modularity, and accessibility. Multimedia content, interactivity of the system, feedback on usability and display design should also be considered. Since the task is fairly complex, more than one author will contribute to the project; therefore learning content management, course management and

(Cont'd)

user rights management (options for access) all have to be coordinated. Although N.N. is familiar with the audience and the intended use for the tutorial, he proposes to test students' prior knowledge by using a survey. The results of the survey will help with design of the modules as they should be able to progress through the tutorial at their own speed and start the tutorial at a level appropriate for them.

The next step in the publishing plan is to determine who will do what, when and how much it will cost. Once the roles are carefully assigned, N.N. prepares authors' contracts and decides on deadlines for completion of particular segments of the project. A publication such as an online tutorial requires a review. N.N. hires at least two reviewers; one is an expert on the content of the tutorial and the other is an expert on learning strategies.

The next tasks are language editing, design and proofreading. Upon completion of these steps, the material is ready for upload to the web (offline), layout and system testing. At this point it is advisable to have a number of students or other intended users test the complete tutorial.

The final version of the tutorial is placed on the library's website and all the students are informed of a new service the library is offering. Students are informed through the library's website and other means of public communication (leaflets, posters, etc.). N.N. continuously collects data on the tutorial usage and records feedback from students for the purposes of future adjustments and updates.

Why publish?

Perhaps it is too bold to say that libraries have strengthened their position with the emergence of electronic publishing. Naturally, from the publishers' point of view, a library has always been a reliable institution. Libraries may have had limitations in information search and retrieval prior to the emergence of computers. Nevertheless, after putting so much effort into and applying knowledge in the advancement of cataloguing and subject cataloguing, librarians have developed the tools for structuring and accessing human knowledge. This expertise today is the basis for metadata structuring and development. We know that each new publication is an addition to the structure and content of human knowledge. Since both publishers and libraries are involved in the building and structuring of human knowledge, a part of libraries' mission falls within the scope of publishing. With each publication every publisher adds to the existing structure and content, as does a library when acting as a publisher. With every new acquisition each library continues to build its collection. Therefore if a library publishes something, it completes both tasks at the same time: adding to its own collection and structuring the global knowledge collection.

This could be a leading criterion when a library decides whether to publish – a unique contribution to completion of the global collection. Such a task should be a part of a national library's, or a consortium of national libraries', mission. Since the advent of the Internet, national libraries have improved their cooperation. *Europeana* is an excellent example.[1]

Not all libraries have such a wide outreach as national libraries. Nevertheless, every single library has its universe, a physical and spiritual territory that belongs to one single library only. And this universe, be it personal, institutional, local, regional or national, is the one that the library has to serve with its publishing production. If the management of a library is aware of this fact, they will have a good criterion to base a decision on what to publish and what not to publish.

Why do libraries publish?

- because they already have the publishing capital;
- for strengthening their position in regard to their users;
- because the librarians' expertise in structuring and accessing human knowledge is a basis for metadata structuring and development;
- because by publishing they build their collections and structure the global knowledge collection;
- because transfer of knowledge and information is a part of their mission;
- for marketing purposes.

Obviously libraries publish for many reasons, but maybe the main reason is to better serve its users. Experienced librarians will easily recognise whether publishing projects are beneficial to their users or not. This is the case with all other library services, and it should be so with publishing. If a library follows this line in its publishing programme, it could hardly go wrong.

Who is the audience for library publications?

Libraries are for readers, said Urquhart (1981), so they also publish for readers. This primarily means that the librarian in charge of publishing must be familiar with the prospective readers. Who are they, what are their needs, preferences, expectations? The library publishing process assumes the interaction between a library/librarian, publishing matter and an audience. In order to choose the publishing matter, the librarian publisher must know the audience, as the readers influence the content, design and format of a publication. This relationship is reciprocal as the publication affects the use of the library's collection and services. The audience and the publishing matter can influence choices, decisions and actions of the library/librarian in a publishing process.

Only excellent teamwork will result in optimal use of library resources, a good product and satisfied customers. Today's audience is global. Its only limitation may be language. If a reader understands the language of an online publication, the accessibility of the published content is worldwide. Distribution of printed publications will be limited by the language and by the distribution channels.

Reception of a publication by an audience to some extent depends on the editorial board. If readers recognise names in the editorial board, they are likely to gain respect for the publication. Even if they do not immediately recognise the names of the experts, they can look them up if the editorial board members' affiliation is published.

The audience can be very diverse. There are at least two different approaches to the audience depending on how familiar the (library) publisher is with the audience. The audience is either known or unknown. For example, if a publisher is preparing a manual on cataloguing rules, she knows her audience will most probably be librarians, or cataloguers to be more specific. This is a known audience. On the other hand, if she is preparing a collection of old geographic maps, or a reprint of old newspapers, her audience will be general, therefore unknown. For an unknown audience a publication has to be edited for the assumed needs and tastes of the audience. Every audience should be approached with respect and the publisher should make every effort to get to know it as best she can. It makes a difference whether a school library publishes children's poetry or artwork to present to their parents and relatives, or reviews of professional books for teachers and fellow librarians, or collections of children's stories recorded from the local oral tradition. The three listed publications will surely differ one from another, not only in their content but also because of the audience for which they were intended. They will also differ in writing style, design, illustrations and publishing format. If it is a story book that is being published, perhaps children will be involved in making it, so their vote at the editorial board might be useful as well.

What do libraries publish?

As already emphasised, libraries have always published. Types of library publications vary depending on the library. Specific characteristics of publishing in relation to the types of the library are discussed in Chapter 7. Publications such as library catalogues, bibliographies and web pages are published by all types of libraries, while some publications are specific to certain types. Library publications may include some of the following:

- catalogues (most often sections of the catalogue related to a certain collection)
- bibliographies, general and special
- journals, bulletins and newsletters
- scholarly publications
- professional papers
- books about distinguished members of a community
- historical reviews or biographies of regionally or locally famous people
- storybooks and picture books by local authors

- children's work
- yearly reports, strategic plans
- website content about the library and its collections
- library blogs
- educational tools for online learning
- tutorials (e.g. information literacy)
- instructions (on how to use library collections or information tools)
- exhibition catalogues
- collections of papers presented at conferences organised by the library
- posters
- press kits
- miscellanea: leaflets, info-materials, invitations.

The complete list of all library publications is much longer than the one above, as libraries produce various publications depending on library type and origin. For example, public libraries in some countries have a major educational role and as such are likely to publish more of educational publications. In other countries, public libraries have more of a cultural role so their publications will probably focus on the cultural life of the community. University libraries will gear more towards scientific publishing such as scholarly papers, conference proceedings, etc.

Print or electronic?

Years ago some professors teaching conservation and preservation of library material would give their students valuable advice: if you want to keep it, print it. Does this advice still hold true? Yes, it does. CDs can break, content can be erased from a server, a company publishing electronic documents can go bankrupt, etc. But if one has printed the text the above-mentioned accidents cannot harm it. For a text of great value, one can create a microfilm of it and have copies stored in different parts of the country or the world. (Is this an old-fashioned outlook? Perhaps so, but this book is not about preservation and conservation.) Still, before making a decision to publish you have to decide whether to do it in print or electronic format. Several points will help you decide: the nature of the future use, the content of the publication, the resources available to the library, and the type of library. All of these issues are important. The content might be static or it might be changing. If the content in question will be accumulating, it means that the printed publication will at some point be outdated. If the content is static, one might consider publishing a book. But we are inclined to say that by its nature, the content of a library's collections is bound to grow, except for some special historical collections, so, if one is presenting content of such a collection, it might be a good decision to print it.

Another consideration is whether today printed publications have a higher reputation and better public image than electronic ones. The way in which the publication will be used is also important. Are the prospective users 'digital-born'? There is a strong inclination of a growing number of users, students in particular, to use electronic publications rather than printed ones. However, this is not true for books of poetry, novels and some textbooks. With the development of interactive learning materials, printed textbooks are losing popularity too. Naturally, generalisations are always dangerous. A librarian in a developing country, or in a country of small language distribution, will look at these issues from a different standpoint than a librarian in a large, developed country. For a small audience with Internet access, print is a less appropriate medium, while a small audience without Internet access will naturally require a printed publication. But then we are generalising again. Perhaps the publisher will find that it is most useful to provide both print and electronic. Consider a librarian who plans to print a catalogue of an exhibition held in his library. If his library has a website, he will take the opportunity to market the event and will place a catalogue on the library website. It will also serve those who do not visit the exhibition. However, at the opening night he will probably not give the visitors a small piece of paper with his library's website address on it. Visitors will expect to get some printed material to guide them through the exhibition. Of course, a website address will be included for those who want more information and who want to further explore the exhibition through links and other content provided on the website. Again, his decision will depend on the nature of the publishing material and on the kind of the library he works in. Publishing in print and electronic medium both have pros and cons regardless of the kind of library, and the decision also depends on the library environment.

Why is an editorial board important?

Although we discuss the editorial board in more detail in Chapter 6 – where we describe various professions involved in the publishing process – we mention it in this part of the book as well because an editorial board holds an important place in creating a publishing plan. The publishing process is teamwork. The process of creating any publication gathers people of many different professions and each has a specific task assigned. Success of the project depends on all links in the chain, from the idea to the finished product. This is why team members should be chosen carefully, both those who will create the content and design and the ones who will work on the production of the final product. And the editorial board has the final word when it comes to decision-making.

What are the tasks of an editorial board? There can be many. At the beginning of a publishing process, its main task is to advise. Regardless of what is to be published, be it print or electronic, it is wise to consult with an editorial board. The reason for this consultation is to get a group of experts to look at the future publishing venture, follow the process of preparation and give their opinion before the publishing process really starts. If the members of the board are chosen wisely, everyone will enjoy working on the project, will learn from each other and at the end will deliver a good product. Members of a publishing board should not be expected to write the planned publication, but to decide on who is going to write. They should not be expected to invent a publication and its content, but to comment and suggest changes to an existing proposal. If there is a good idea related to the project, it should be discussed with the editorial board. If the idea is not so good, it is again important to have the editorial board help with reconsidering the idea and discussing further steps.

The library director, or a librarian in charge of publication (we also consider web pages to be a publication), should be careful when selecting members of an editorial board. The person who decides who the members of the board will be should be well acquainted with prospective members' careers and trust their references. It is not necessary that future members know one another personally, but the librarian in charge of publishing should be familiar with them, or should consult someone who is. Retired experts are excellent sources of such information, including retired editors or directors of publishing houses or libraries. Why is this? The experience they gained in their professional career is invaluable. They have worked with many professionals and have met them in real-life situations. Once the board is well assembled, the members are ready to decide on the fate of a received proposal. They will be able to decide whether to publish or not, who will be involved in publishing, what the scope of the publication will be and so on.

It is advisable to keep editorial boards small in size. Three to five individuals who are willing to commit to the task should be sufficient. Large, interdisciplinary projects may be an exception, where the members of the board may have to be specialists in various disciplines.

The publishing plan

No project should be conducted without a precise plan. Most publishers normally have a publishing plan. The publishing plan is a list of titles that are going to be published in a certain time period, usually a year. This list is spread out throughout a calendar year depending on the publisher's profile. Trade publishers will adjust their plan to events such as Easter, Christmas, summer holidays, and textbook publishers to the beginning of the academic year. Libraries as publishers will have different factors that will determine their publishing schedule. Library publishing is often related to various library events such as anniversaries, exhibitions and special events. Generally, there is one fundamental difference between libraries as publishers and other publishers. As a rule library publishing is in some way related to its collections because a library uses publishing as means to better accomplish its mission. Through publishing, a library is promoting its collections in a different way than merely by building it and making records available to the users. Librarians are also often emotionally invested in their collections. Who could prepare an exhibition on, for example, rare books and publish a catalogue for it better than a librarian who has spent many days working with this collection?

With the advent of online publishing, libraries' graphic collections have become more attractive.

Joint library publishing projects where a number of libraries work together presenting pieces from their collections is adding new value. Such joint publications could potentially save the users travelling and browsing time.

Drawing up a publishing plan is often a result of well-coordinated teamwork because it involves making a series of decisions. Although it seems to be merely a list of publications to be produced within a certain time period, it actually implies decisions made on issues such as human, material and financial resources. A sound publishing plan will ensure that time and money are not wasted.

Timetable

A timetable is a simple and efficient way to achieve publishing goals on time. We suggest starting at the end – the public presentation of a publication. Working backwards the publisher will be able to plan all the necessary steps and adjust all the previous steps to meet the final deadline. Table 5.1 provides an example.

Work that precedes the moment when the editor receives a manuscript and the time needed to complete each step both depend on the type of text and the entire decision-making process (from the idea to the selection of manuscripts/authors).

Table 5.1   Example timetable

December 15	Public presentation
December 10	Delivery from the printer
November 15	Approval
November 10	3rd proofreading completed
November 1	2nd proofreading completed
October 20	1st proofreading completed
October 10	Layout completed
September 10	Graphic editor and/or designer starts
August 20	Language editing starts
August 1	Review (if planned) starts
July 15	Editor starts to work on the manuscript
July 15	Author delivers the manuscript

If the text is to be reviewed, additional time needs to be allocated for the reviewing and editing process before the manuscript is sent for further processing.

This timetable is purely illustrative because the time allocations depend on the length and complexity of the manuscript.

Making such a timetable for each publication, while assigning the tasks to skilled staff, will result in a high-quality publication that will be completed on time. If time is short, and this happens often, a publisher has to keep a close watch on the timetable and schedule regular checkpoints more often than when there is plenty of time. One should be very careful with the printing houses. If time is short, printing should be done at a reliable printer's with whom the publisher has done business in the past. If there is plenty of time before the deadline, a publisher may search for and choose a different printer. When communicating with the printer, one should always insist on receiving a print dummy[2] before committing to print.

If a text is published in an electronic format, additional time should be allocated for technical issues such as uploading to a website and testing the software, planning and testing the navigation and assessing the overall functionality. Although it may seem that these are totally technical issues, they are not. The way a publication is accessed, i.e. on the web, will depend on its purpose, content and the audience for which it was intended. Both layout design and navigation design are not only technical processes but also creative ones. All of these issues should be considered before handing the publication off to web programmers to put it up on the web.

During the whole process library publishers should keep marketing in mind. The marketing process of either print or electronic publications should begin before it is published and continue after it is published.

Financial plan

'Money makes the world go round!' Fortunately, or perhaps unfortunately, this is true for every single publishing project. Publishing is probably one of the few human activities that has mainly been supported by donations because books have always been considered to serve noble purposes (although some purposes were not so noble and very often they were for personal gain and strengthening influence). Regardless of this, every publishing project must have a financial plan. No project should be started before this plan is clear and final, because no matter how good the project is, it can fail if the finances fail. This is true for every publishing project.

A library publisher must anticipate all possible expenses before deciding to publish something. One can choose from two different approaches: a financial plan for each particular publication, or a financial plan based on all of the publishing activities, something like a general financial publishing plan. The second approach does not eliminate the need for estimating the cost of each publication at each stage of the process, because, at the end, it is all a part of the same library budget.

Usually, library publishing projects are of some importance for the community, so libraries often apply for financial support to their founders or governing bodies. Often libraries will use resources from their own budget and combine them with sponsorship or donations. Regardless of where the funding comes from, a library needs to know the estimated budget needed to produce a publication. A library should know the budget for the publication it intends to publish even before it applies for funding. Generally, a financial plan has to be submitted with every request for a donation or any other kind of financial support. Also, when a project is completed, a report has to be sent to all donors. It is very important that all projects that receive donations are completed in due time. One should be careful when submitting a request for funding. In some cases it is up to the applicant to set the timeframe in which the publishing project will be completed, and it is wise to plan carefully here. It should be kept in mind that it always takes more time than anticipated, so just as with the expenses, it is always a good idea to have some extra time/money available.

Every publisher tries to keep publishing costs low, otherwise the final product will be too expensive, it will not sell, and there will be no profit. Although libraries do not publish for profit, it is helpful to make some. The gain most libraries expect from publishing is often measured by criteria other than financial profit. This depends on the library's reasons for publishing. If a library publishes information material or an education tool for its users, the library's primary gain is fulfilment of its mission in serving and benefiting the readers. If a library publishes proceedings from a conference, the money made from the sales can go towards covering the publishing expenses, or it may even be left over as a profit to be reinvested in a future publishing project. However, as with any publication, the goal is to keep publishing costs reasonable and based on 'value for money'.

Some phases of a publishing project are more expensive than others. Start-up or set-up costs are usually higher than printing or dissemination costs. This is because more work goes into creating the content (advising, authors' costs, etc.), workflows, editing, graphic design and layout. Even when most of this work is done pro bono, there are still expenses such as staff time or equipment.

If publishing costs cannot be covered, libraries very often decide to change the format and publish electronically, because it drastically cuts down on delivery costs. Sometimes a decision to do this happens along the way, for example when support from a partner or other source of funding fails. For this reason it is always a good idea to have the materials prepared in such a way that they are easily repurposed for digital publishing. One of the major arguments for electronic publishing over print is the lower cost of publishing, especially if open-source software is used. Many steps in publication preparation are automated, there are no costs of printing, and search engines facilitate marketing of the publication, which also decreases project costs.

However, when deciding whether to print or publish electronically, cost should not be the only deciding factor. Readers' point of view should also be considered. If the future publication is intended for a small number of readers and therefore will be printed in a small print run, the unit cost for such a publication will be high. However, if the potential readers have no Internet access or have a poor one, printing the particular publication is still the only way to reach these readers.

Regardless of the final decision on the format – print or electronic – it is imperative to set up a publishing budget before the project goes into implementation.

In Table 5.2, the example of a budget is given for a printed publication, as was the timetable in Table 5.1.

Table 5.2   Publication budget

Technical characteristics

Format	17 × 24 cm (6.7 inch × 9.5 inch)
Printing	1/1
Paper	80 gr/m2
Binding	Hard cover
Number of pages	300
Layout	Provided by the library in PDF
Print run	500
Packing	Boxes (20 books in a box)
Delivery	Customer address

Budget, in EUR

Expenses	
Author's honorarium	2,000
Editing	800
Language editing	500
Graphic editing	1,000
Cover design	500
Layout	800
Printing and binding	2,800
Total (8,400/500 = 16.80)	8,400
Income *	14,000 (earnings = 5,600)
Subsidy from the city government	1,000
Subsidy from the county (or state) government	1,500
Library's own investment	3,000
Sold by subscription (50 copies at 20 EUR per copy)	1,000

* Sales planned on the market (250 copies at 30 EUR per copy = 7,500)

When calculating revenues and earnings, the following must be taken into account:

- 5,600 EUR revenue is not earnings because the library invested 3,000 EUR of its own funds.

- The unit revenue of 30 EUR per copy can be earned only if the library itself is a distributer to the end buyer, in other words if the publication is sold at the library. Otherwise, if the publication is distributed through, for example, bookstores, expected mark-up is usually a minimum of 30%, and the library's earnings should be reduced by that amount.

In most cases libraries try to earn the return on their investment. Extra profit is welcomed but is not the sole purpose for publishing.

Based on estimations, which differ from one sort of publication to another (i.e. black and white illustrations instead of colour), the library can decide to publish in print or electronic format and to monitor the costs during the publishing process.

Last but not least, monitoring of expenditure should be entrusted to a single person. This could be an editor or a manager, or someone in whom the management has confidence. Expenses should be carried out according to the financial plan and should be approved before the money is spent. Sometimes, adjustments are needed, but in most cases this means higher costs than initially anticipated. This scenario is possible because, for example, the manuscript needs to be longer than originally planned, or there is a need for more illustrations because interesting new material was discovered during the research, etc. Since the expenses need to be balanced with the budget, constant attention needs to be given to the financial plan.

Manuscript selection

Once the need for publishing has been determined, the audience identified and there is an idea of the final publication, what is missing is a manuscript.

There are two main ways of manuscript acquisition. One is for a publisher to commission a manuscript and another is for an author to offer it to a publisher. It does not happen very often that authors offer manuscripts to a library. They are more likely to go to a publisher. As we said before, by publishing something a library wants to fulfil its mission to better serve its patrons and the library staff are most likely to know best how publishing can help accomplish this goal. This is why a library is most likely to commission a manuscript, a script or a scenario for something it wants to publish. Often a writer will be found among the librarians, especially in larger libraries. Librarians are usually methodical and patient. These two characteristics along with plenty of books for inspiration are excellent prerequisites for writing a manuscript. However, as with any other professional publishing situation, the manuscript delivery deadline should be set well in advance and agreed upon by the librarian who will be the author. Naturally, if no one on the staff is available or willing to write a desired manuscript, the author needs to be found elsewhere. It can be done informally through word of mouth or formally through a call for proposals. At a university or a special library, an author may be sought out among professors or experts at the company. Since libraries serve user communities and the theme of the publication will most likely be based on the library's collection, there is a significant chance that the potential writer can be found at the same campus or company. So in fact, an author needs to be selected, not a manuscript. Again, a library is better off than a trade publisher who has to look for a manuscript on the market. The library is likely to be well acquainted with the potential writer, as well as with their writing style and field of interest. A public library can also look for a writer in the community it serves. In this respect university libraries are in the best position because they work in an environment where writing is the everyday task of most employees.

After the potential author (or authors) is chosen, a list of their tasks should be carefully agreed on. The agreement between a library as a publisher and the potential author should be very precise. It is best to provide an outline of the publication with the table of contents, as well as guidelines and instructions. This way a potential author will better understand the context and the vision of the publication, which is especially important if the call for proposals is for writing separate chapters of a book. Also, a publisher will have a clear picture of the future manuscript and it will be easier to determine the length of each chapter and consequently that of the whole book. Clear guidelines on length, layout and format can guarantee that all submitted chapters will be uniform, which makes the editor's work easier.

Collections managers should be included in the meetings with potential authors because they might make useful suggestions on various aspects of the content. This is especially important when it comes to the search for illustrations. Collection managers are acquainted with the content of their collections and with the physical status of items. They can also advise on the best way to make the reproduction needed for preparing the layout and can provide the best possible camera-ready document. The author might need documents from other libraries or from museums or archives from other countries. This is the case in Europe, for example, where countries have often changed rulers, and cities changed countries, throughout history. If a library is the publisher, another library, museum or archive is likely to provide the needed documents at no cost or at the minimal reproduction cost. Professional solidarity plays a role here.

Now, after the need for a publication is identified, choosing an author is the next and very important step in the publishing project. The following checklist can help with the selection of the right person:

- **a reference list:** looking up who the potential authors have already worked with and what their projects were; ideally, speaking to the references personally;

- **communication skills:** e-mail correspondence and a telephone conversation are useful, but a face-to-face conversation is highly desirable;

- **list of publications:** what the potential author has already published;

- **word of mouth:** gathering information from trustworthy people.

It is unlikely that the wrong person will be selected if all of the above checks give positive results. However, publishers have to be prepared for all unforeseen obstacles, which means they have to be flexible. It seems like a dark scenario, but it happens: the author doesn't meet the deadline, their work is not delivered according the agreed standards, the author did not understand the point and the manuscript needs to be completely rewritten, etc.

Authors' contracts

The author or the editor of the project has been selected. If this is someone from the library staff, the library manager can simply allocate a part of that employee's working hours to the project. If this is not possible, extra hours can be compensated for separately. Whatever the arrangement, it needs to be written down and signed. Also, it needs to be stated what happens if a person resigns before the job is completed. It must be ensured that the project will be completed on time. It is very useful to write down the timetable. This will help the author and the publisher. The first draft of a manuscript is a critical point and it should be delivered well ahead of a deadline so that there is time left for corrections and amendments. If the draft is not delivered on time, this is a cause for alarm and the author should be contacted to check what the problem is.

As far as copyright is concerned the institution's rules should be followed, but an effort should be made to agree for the library to be the owner of the rights. With appropriate compensation, authors should agree.

A contract should contain the following elements:

- title and subtitle of the future publication;
- length of the manuscript (expressed in number of words);
- deadline (and consequences for not meeting it – usually parties agree on a new deadline, but if the author fails to meet it again for any reason, the contract should be terminated – the conditions for breaking a contract should be stated in advance);
- technical description of how the manuscript will be delivered and its format;
- copyright issues (also copyright for alternative formats);
- reprints, translations and new editions;
- royalties (if manuscript will be paid and publisher expects the profit);
- author's copies.

The contract should satisfy both parties, because the author is more likely to work with enthusiasm and hence deliver a good manuscript.

Layout

Imagine yourself in front of a bookshop window or browsing an online bookstore. A book cover is what attracts us or keeps us from entering a bookshop or from continuing to browse the web pages about a certain book. In many cases this is important if we are not looking for a specific title. But even if we look for a specific title, it is much more pleasurable to buy or borrow a book that will give us aesthetic satisfaction. The design of a book cover is one of the tasks of a graphic designer. Often publishers assign book cover design to a different graphic designer than the one who designs the layout. This decision is usually made by the editor and the goal is to have the most attractive cover possible.

The choice of format of a book will also be an important decision to make. The format serves the purpose of the book. This is much more true for printed books, but for both print and electronic the layout of the pages is what an expert reader will pay attention to, and for others it can be an important factor in attacting readers' interest. The issue of layout and book covers applies to each title separately but also to a series of titles, where there has to be a uniform appearance but each unit has to have its own feel. When it comes to a series it is even more important to think about design and book cover, because frequent changes are not good – a series must have a recognisable identity and look.

The above factors should be considered carefully and it is very important to request a print dummy from the graphic designer or a studio. It is imperative to not skip this phase.

One must be cautious never to agree on a different format from the one seen on a dummy. It should be in real size because this is the only way to make the right decision about the layout. The same procedure should be followed for electronic publications. An offline version should always be submitted for approval before the publication is completed. In both cases, this is a great responsibility and a lot of work because it is the publisher's job to brief the graphic designer in detail in order to produce the best possible product. This means that the publisher must have clear ideas of what needs to be done.

A graphic designer will want to know about the target audience. They might not be as familiar with the audience as the librarian publishers are.

A publisher should take part in the selection of illustrations. Collecting the illustrations to be published is sometimes a designer's responsibility and sometimes the author's, but in many cases a conscientious publisher will be involved in the selection of illustrations as well. This is an exciting and interesting task, but it requires a lot of practical knowledge. One must keep in mind that most non-fiction books are read or consulted by experts. This means that a new book must bring new information and – in the case of illustrations – new and yet unpublished ones.

The same goes for textbooks. Before recommending them to students, a teacher or professor will carefully examine the content. And finally there is the general audience, which should never be underestimated. When creating a book, printed or electronic, the most knowledgeable and most critical reader must always be considered. A publisher should think of a reader who is an expert in the field and also of the most critical reviewers. Consequently, a publisher can advise the graphic designer and together they can make good decisions.

Print publishing

How would one describe a printing house? As an industry with a soul? A finishing touch of the publishing project? Whatever the case may be, the printing house is the last station before the book starts its journey towards a reader. Dealing with printing houses before high-tech times was always an adventure. Why so? Because very often the print shop employees had different tastes or a different idea about, for example, the paper that was to be used, the intensity of the colours, and the kind of binding. The best results were achieved when a fair compromise was reached between the publisher represented by the designer and the printer who cared about his reputation and respected the customer. But these times are long gone. In the late 1970s, depending on geographic location, a new technology was introduced to the printing industry. This change started when computers replaced lead trays for text setting and with this the manufacturing era in printing became history.

Today, computers are used in all aspects of the printing process as well as in running a printing house. Consequently the relationship to customers changed as well. In the past, after the agreement about the price of printing was reached, the production phase began by delivering a manuscript to the *metre*, a professional who was in charge of setting. The delivery was usually done by the graphic editor, who would then choose a typeface. Today, there is no need to go to the printing house in person. Usually a publisher deposits a camera-ready layout onto the printing house server. Shortly afterwards, the printing house will deliver a dummy for possible corrections. If the layout was done carefully, hopefully the only thing to do at this point is to sign the dummy off and send it back to the printer. If there are mistakes to be corrected, the procedure has to be repeated, until the publisher is completely satisfied with the dummy. The signed dummy will be kept in the printer's archives, as a proof of the order. In case the customer is not satisfied with the outcome, the dummy will be the *corpus delicti*. Therefore the dummy needs to be carefully inspected because the corrections are relatively easy and inexpensive to make in this phase of production, but once the book is printed it is too late. Nevertheless, mistakes do happen. If they are minor mistakes, the publisher will print a leaflet called *errata corrige* and in this way inform a reader about the mistakes.

Regardless of all of the e-mails and servers, a customer should visit the print shop every once in a while, especially if it is a local one. Nothing can substitute for face-to-face conversation. This is important for good business relations but it will also benefit the product. If the publication is demanding, the publisher's personal attention might be necessary when choosing the printing paper or looking through the examples of binding. On rare occasions, the publisher will be invited to be by the printing press when the first sheets of paper are printed. While the press is running, the publishers are able to inspect the result. If everything is as it should be, they can sit back, relax and wait for several days to receive the finished book. New technologies have enormously increased the speed and reliability of the printing presses. The automation of binding has followed suit, so now printers are able to produce high-quality products in a short time. Regardless of this, one should make sure that when an order is placed, a delivery deadline and terms of payment are agreed. It is convenient to have one's *own* printing house. But still, before printing each new publication, one should go and check the prices with at least two other printers if time permits. This is not because the usual printing house cannot be trusted, but simply because the price depends on many factors – mainly technology, the quantity of work the printer has to deliver in a certain period, the prices of paper they have in stock. Since the price of printing is one of the highest items in the publishing budget, every bit saved can be used for producing another publication.

Libraries today outsource more demanding printing projects. However, libraries in the past have often had in-house binderies with print shops, used mostly for collection preservation and for simple printing jobs. Building on this tradition, libraries still keep these binderies and are improving the print shops, where new technologies play an important role facilitating simple and small print jobs in limited editions. On the other hand, new technologies are also marginalising the print shops because they provide an alternative way of publishing without printing; electronic publishing does not need a print shop. In this very fact many see a way to save time and money.

Electronic publishing

It is our opinion that even in the distant future, printed and electronic publications will continue to coexist. The balance between the two might change depending on the environment of the user and we will witness an increase in electronic publication, especially in the academic environment, as described below.

Johnson and Luther (2007: 9), reporting about the study conducted by the US Association of Research Libraries, stress that 'the users have voted – and they want the convenience of electronic'. The study has shown that libraries can deliver a higher level of service with electronic resources, and libraries take this into consideration when offering digital journal subscriptions. Librarians believe that with this shift towards e-only journals they can raise the quality of services, reduce subscription fees and lower the cost of production and delivery.

So these are the trends in research libraries where there is a great need for on-time and up-to-date information. This is also proof that computer experts and librarians are working hand in hand.

Taking this technological advancement into account, Brown et al. (2007) predict a radical change in the publishing industry. They believe that usage patterns have changed dramatically and that many scholars are increasingly relying on electronic information sources in their research and teaching:

> Transformation on the creation and production sides is taking longer, but ultimately may have an even more profound impact on the way scholars work. Publishers have made progress putting their legacy content online, especially with journals. We believe the next stage will be the creation of new formats made possible by digital technologies, ultimately allowing scholars to work in deeply integrated electronic research and publishing environments that will enable real-time dissemination, collaboration, dynamically-updated content, and usage of new media. (Brown et al. 2007: 4)

In most countries libraries are networked and in many cases they form a library system, meaning that a user of any library can benefit from the services of all or most libraries in the system, sometimes even worldwide. It is also a fact that the open-access movement has been embraced by many libraries because free use of knowledge is one of the main principles of libraries. This is why librarians look at electronic publishing as a way to better fulfil their essential mission, but they will continue to collect, preserve and enable the use of printed publications for the very same reason. Of course the balance between print and electronic will be in proportion to the population of users they serve and in accordance with their geographical location and economic and cultural environment.

Distribution by the library

All elements of a publishing chain are important, and so is distribution. There is no sense in publishing unless the end results are distributed to readers, whether by selling them or lending at a library. For this reason distribution assumes two main tasks: marketing and physical delivery. Without effective marketing the audience might never find out about the publication, in which case the physical delivery will not be necessary and all the money and effort of publishing will be wasted. That is why when making a publishing plan marketing time and expense must be included.

One way to distribute publications is through a library. In regard to sales, most libraries have two types of publication: the ones that are distributed free of charge and those that are intended for sale. One must keep in mind that even the publications that are distributed free of charge to the end user will still cost the library the storage and distribution.

Of course, almost every library is able to exhibit all its publications in public spaces where patrons can see them and, if interested, buy. This is fairly easy to organise, but is not enough. On a library's website there can be a page where all publications are displayed along with prices and information on ordering or subscribing. This is a convenient way to reach the patrons of one particular library but not the general public. The limitation of this marketing method is that this page will be looked at by the patrons of this library but not others. It is important to assign someone at the library to be in charge of distribution; for example, a librarian who works in the interlibrary loan department, who already has experience in receiving and delivering publications, could devote a part of their time to the sale of publications. If this is not possible, the success will be limited. The librarian in charge of sales can also be responsible for announcing new publications, making a web and printed catalogue of the publications, updating the web page with information about new publications and organising presentations. These tasks can also be assigned to more than one person in the library. Other libraries, academic institutions, schools, bookstores and retailers can be notified of the arrival of a new publication through e-mail distribution lists or through regular postal services. The distribution is an important and time-consuming task and it has to be done continuously. With electronic publications the situation is different. The library can charge a fee per viewing or downloading of a publication, or charge a subscription fee in case of periodical publications. A good description of these options is given by the Ithaka report: 'Alongside these changes in content creation and publication, alternative distribution models (institutional repositories, pre-print servers, open access journals) have also arisen with the aim to broaden access, reduce costs, and enable open sharing of content' (Brown, Griffiths and Rascoff, 2007: 6). Brown et al. stress that economic models vary according to types of content and audience. They believe that different marketplaces for publishing various contents will continue '. . . from fee-based to open access, from peer reviewed to self-published, from single author to collaboratively created, from simple text to rich media' (Brown et al., 2007: 6) and will include commercial and not-for-profit entities. Thus, the collaboration among libraries, publishers and academic computing centres should be included.

Distribution by a retailer

A library may decide to entrust the distribution of its publications to a retailer. The reasons can vary: lack of personnel, lack of storage space, or lack of technological support. In such cases a library will decide to hire a retailer.

An advantage to this method is that the library is not undertaking this important task. The disadvantage is that it costs money. Retailers will ask for a rebate that will not be lower than 30 per cent of the price of the publication. But the task will probably be done efficiently and the library staff will have more time to work on other projects. It might be possible to negotiate a lower rebate if an exclusive retailer is used. This means that no one but this retailer will have the right to distribute the publications. If the retailer does not have the exclusive rights, the request for the rebate will surely be higher. The rebate is the highest if the retailer buys the publications in advance. This means that the retailer is taking the responsibility for the future sales to individual customers. The most usual arrangement with retailers is sale on commission, which means that the library will be paid only for the publications that are sold. The library and the retailer will agree about the intervals in which the payments to the library are to be made.

Some independent publishers that have only a few employees usually sell their products through retailers. Here again all the pros and cons must be weighed up and a decision needs to be made whether to distribute through the library or through a retailer.

Notes

1. Available from: *http://www.europeana.eu* (accessed 5 August 2010).

2. 'Print dummy' is the final prototype of the future publication to a scale of 1:1 and it is intended for final proofreading of text, illustrations, captions and layout. The purpose of a print dummy is for a publisher to get a clear idea of the final product and for a printer as an approval by the customer because the publisher signs off on the print dummy and by doing this gives it a go-head for printing. With more demanding or complicated publications, the printer will require the publisher to sign off on each signature and sometimes on each page.

6

Basic professions in publishing applied to library publishing

Abstract: Publishing is a complex activity that involves a number of highly skilled professionals, such as editor, graphic editor, designer, language editor, proofreader, etc. Therefore, coordination and teamwork are necessary as well as an organised set of procedures that leads to a successful final product – a publication. This chapter describes the key professions that are part of the publishing process, considered from the library publisher's point of view. All procedures have to be performed by skilled professionals regardless of whether some of them will be outsourced or done in-house.

Key words: basic publishing professionals, adding value, editor, reviewer, translator, designer, proofreader

Publishing as adding value

From the initial idea to procuring a manuscript to the delivery of a finished product to the readers (Figure 6.1), the position of a publisher entails a series of tasks along the way, from the market for a manuscript to the market outlet for placement of the finished product. This process includes numerous professions. Although this schema is primarily aimed at commercial publishers, it applies to library publishers as well. The difference with libraries as publishers is that their main goal of selling is not making profit; rather, it is ensuring

Figure 6.1 Publishing as adding value[1]

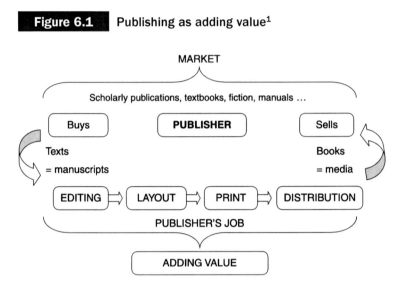

access to the publications to those for whom it is intended. However, whether it is a commercial publisher or not, the effort is usually made to recover the invested money. Often donations are used in order to lower the price of the publication so it becomes affordable for more people. This especially holds true for underdeveloped and developing countries where a book is rarely a priority on which to spend money.

The publisher's mission is to add value to the initial product – the manuscript – through editing, formatting, printing (if the publication is in print) and distributing. All of these jobs are done by experts that require excellent and coordinated work from the editor to the proofreader and from the printers to the distributers. The publisher is responsible for all stages, from the initial one to the final product. Adding value has always been the publisher's task and this is especially so in this day of electronic publishing. The fact that in the chain of information mediating libraries add value, and publishing is a part of this, makes them an additional important player in the publishing arena. Concise description of the importance of adding value in the electronic environment while emphasising the importance of providing navigation and authority is given by Mark Bide:

> The network reduces the effective distance between author and reader, and at the same time reduces the barriers to entry for those who seek to mediate the chain that links them. All of those who currently provide mediation services are under pressure – and none have any absolute right to maintain their current position. They must continue to add value – or they will disappear. (Bide, 2002: 60)

Bide believes that all who participate in placement of information, including libraries and publishers, in the electronic environment must continue to use the same models for adding value as the ones used in the physical environment, although their relative importance might not be the same. He predicts that access and aggregation will become less important while the navigation and authority will gain in importance. He also believes that those contributors to the value chain who provide navigation and authority will become key factors in future evaluation of the value chain by the users, and those are the exact values that libraries are already developing as a part of their regular work.

Publisher

Many authors believed that with the advent of electronic publishing, the role of a publisher would be diminished or would disappear. The well-known role of a gatekeeper will no longer create problems and every author will be able to publish whatever he or she wishes. However, publishing is a process and it has a very specific role in society. Authority and relevance of publications are very important to readers. Who establishes the authority? A publisher. How does a reader recognise the authority and relevance of a published work? By having trust in a publisher. This relationship between the publisher and its readership is a carefully constructed network of relations that is passed on from generation to generation.

It is true that today, in the times of electronic media, anyone can publish. However, those who do have to be aware that the reputation they earn can be one of trust and respect or the opposite. Publishers' success in the market depends on the respect of readers, whoever those readers might be.

Thomas Woll (1999) stresses that publishers have a higher chance of success if they develop and abide by the C3 principles – commitment, consistency and credibility. They have to be committed to their project, work systematically and consistently in all phases of the process and develop good relations with readers/customers.

Formally speaking, the publisher is responsible for any problems that might arise with the publication, in regard to content or legal procedures. There is a need to distinguish a publisher as a person and a publisher as an institution.

Independent publishers (small and alternative publishers) are usually represented by a person, often the owner of the publishing house. If this is the case then he or she will be responsible for all the work (organisational, financial and publishing) within the publishing house.

Since trade publishers are often big companies, they usually have a board of directors. In such companies it has to be decided who will take the responsibility. Often it is a president of the board, but it can be decided differently.

With scholarly publishers, university presses, universities and similar institutions, responsibilities can be assigned in a variety of ways. Often the secretary general of an organisation assumes the legal responsibility for the publisher, especially when publishing is not the organisation's principal activity. Libraries as publishers function as publishing companies, although there may be just one person responsible for the whole process. This makes the role of the editorial board acting primarily as an advisory body even more important, but it is also possible that its members take on responsibilities in the publishing process (such as writing the manuscript or some parts of it, reviewing, monitoring the process, accepting a publishing plan, etc.).

Editorial board

Every institution dealing with publishing must have a specific publishing direction. This direction will be a result of the basic social character of the institution. It is necessary to form an editorial board so they can frame the publishing direction into a publishing policy based on their understanding of the basic social role of its parent institution. Naturally, an editorial board is not one person, but we could say it is a collective person. If the editorial board manages to work well as a team, superior results can be expected. The quality of the final product may depend on the quality of teamwork of the editorial board. The teamwork itself is not visible from the outside but it is reflected in the impact the publisher has on the book market, since everything that has to do with the manuscript is happening in the editorial board. A library too can establish an editorial board, which might consist of librarians who are interested in publishing or are assigned to it by their management according to their capabilities and professional background. Of course, its success will depend on many circumstances, such as the number of permanent staff working in the library, the budget that can be allocated to publishing, the overall policy towards publishing, type of library, and management's commitment to publishing. Whether the editorial board is similar to the one in a publishing house, or it is a small group of professionals in charge of publishing, it is a place where the content of a publication is decided on.

The technical part of the process (graphic editing, layout) will often be outsourced in order to have the work done professionally. It is wrong to believe that a computer and a systems librarian or a librarian who in their spare time likes playing with layouts can do a good job. Graphic design is an art, or rather an applied art, and a professional should be hired to do it. If a graphic designer, perhaps from another company, can become a part of the team, the results are even better. There is one reliable way to find out whether a prospective graphic designer is a real professional. One should try to find out whether they have read the manuscript. If they did, it is a sure sign of dedication. If they did not, they might miss the main point of the manuscript. If possible, the management should assign an office within a library to be used for publishing activities. This could be a place where the editorial board meets, authors come in for an interview, and where all library publications could be exhibited. However, most libraries lack space so this request might be difficult to fulfil. Whatever the case, it is good to always hold meetings in the same room. Space is important because people concentrate better if they are in a familiar place. If a group of people meets on a regular basis, they tend sit in the same place and next to the same person every time. There are several reasons for this but the one that is important to us is that people feel at ease in their regular places. When people are at ease they think better and have better ideas, and to produce a good publication there needs to be plenty of good ideas. Nowadays many editorial boards meet only electronically, because budget cuts are so severe that most publishers do not want to pay for face-to-face meetings, not even once a year. Teleconferencing can help, but there should be a common electronic platform to help with communications while working on a publishing project. This practice is most common in journal editing. However, if the members of the editorial board are mainly staff from the same library, there is no reason not to have face-to-face meetings whenever needed or regularly, depending on the type of publications being prepared. In fact, we are of the opinion that a library editorial board can behave as an independent publisher because it is more mission than market driven. Some authors, such as Owen (1996), who analyse the position of independent publishers in book markets, believe that publishing conglomerates cannot reach the level of quality that independent publishers reach because of the lack of orientation towards the mission, commitment to collaborating with authors, and consistency of publishing policy because their main goal is to succeed in the market. Although Owen's statement dates from more than 15 years ago, today's trend in merging into publishing conglomerates is now confirming his words. Libraries as publishers have characteristics of independent publishers because of the low staff turnover, and the possibility of continuous supervision of all segments of production. They are not dependent on the market and are very mission oriented.

Editor

In book production, the role of editor is a crucial one. Even if detailed arrangements with the author are made, there will be the need for an editor. Of course, this task can be assigned to a librarian responsible for the publishing process, but it should be done with caution as the person in the editor's role needs to be very familiar with the content as well as with managing a publishing process. The intellectual and organisational contribution of the editor is enormous and in complex publications the editor is the only person who at all times knows what is going on with the publication. The graphic editor, the illustrator and the photographer are all a part of the team, but the editor is the person who should have control over the entire process and coordinate all of the elements that have to be put together. It rarely happens that the first draft of the manuscript submitted by an author remains unchanged. In most cases it is the editor who works on the changes with the author.

Institutions in culture or science have been known to entrust to one of their employees the making of the entire publication, especially when it comes to anniversary editions. In such cases one person collects the materials, writes the text, labels the illustrations and edits the entire issue. Thanks to the omnipresence of computers, setting the layout is often added to this series of expert tasks. Such a way of conducting projects seems unprofessional and will often cause errors and the need for corrections. In the case of joint authorship, the editor's work might take more time and is more complex because there are more authors to work with. In most cases the author likes to get a publisher's opinion before submitting a final version of the manuscript.

From what has been said up to this point, it should be obvious that from the very start the work on a publishing project is based on an intensive interaction between the author and the publisher or editor. If the editor and the author are 'on the same page', the project has a good chance to be successful. The editor's role is even more important if the publisher moves on to a new publishing project. Since libraries are looking to the future, long-term projects are perfectly suited for this environment. In this case the editor's role is not only to coordinate the work on one manuscript but to envision the concept of the whole project.

Working on a manuscript is only the first step in the publishing process. This part of work is exciting and often very demanding. Some authors have ventured into editing and as a consequence they understand that a publication needs to be a part of an existing context. Every publication makes an impact on the publisher's profile and for libraries as publishers this is just as true. A reader recognises the relevance of a published work by trusting the publisher's reputation. The same is true for an editor because the status and relevance of a publication often depend on the editor's reputation.

In publishing houses editors are influential, responsible, highly professional individuals with rich work experience. It is important to be careful with the choice of an editor, as with the choice of an author. The editor has to have a broad education, good communication skills and many professional relations. Such an editor will be able to work with authors on equal footing, which is crucial for the success of the project, and it ensures that the author accepts the editor's suggestions, which can sometimes be challenging.

Of course, editors' tasks vary from one project to another, but the most important thing is that they are proficient in editing so they are able to make the initial evaluation of a manuscript that will eventually be reviewed. In publishing conglomerates, editors are organised by the subject field they are editing. In independent publishing houses there might be only one editor, but in that case it will specialise in a certain field. A librarian could become a good editor if they know the collection well and have an interest in publishing. Enthusiasm for and interest in a certain topic are essential prerequisites for being a good editor. If an expert has sufficient background knowledge in the field, with some advice from an experienced editor he or she can do a fairly good editing job. People become editors in different ways, but most commonly by experience and by gradual advancement in the profession. Editors' tasks should be to stimulate a creative atmosphere and teamwork within the editorial office, looking for and procuring manuscripts, keeping track of new titles in foreign languages that might be of interest for translation, attending book fairs, and keeping contact with writers, newspapers and other media. Naturally, within a library, especially if it is the librarians who are in charge of publishing, all of these activities will be modified in order to fit the library's mission.

Graphic editor

Many publications are illustrated. Collecting illustrations is as important as the work on a manuscript for both print and electronic publications. Depending on the subject of the book, readers expect illustrations regardless of the format. Libraries are at a vast advantage over other publishers when it comes to collecting illustrations. In many cases they have the material at hand. Take for example old newspapers. Many graphic editors use copyright-free old newspapers as an excellent source of illustrations, especially when dealing with books on history. Often the author of a manuscript will collect and deliver the illustrations that are needed, but in many cases the editor or the graphic editor will look for additional illustrations. That is when a search for images starts. All publishers want their editions to have high-quality illustrations and are looking for original material not yet published. This is a matter of publishers' prestige. This is why graphic editors work with libraries, archives and museums but also with collectors, especially of old postcards, which can be very useful, not only as an excellent source of illustrations but also as a source of information, as are photographs, maps, plans, drawings. The search for images can take a long time and be very demanding. If the images cannot be found in-house, they have to be located elsewhere and reproduction permission needs to be sought.

Public institutions will usually cede the material free of charge to non-profit publishers and charge commercial publishers according to the regular price list. Sometimes a graphic editor will look for an illustrator or a painter in order to commission a drawing of what is needed. Placement of accurately labelled illustrations in well-laid-out text creates a new and rich content and adds value to the manuscript and to the illustration itself. Unfortunately, a reader cannot have the insight into all the potential illustrative material because the editors have made a selection. With electronic publishing, where a lot more material can be published because of less concern about the volume of the publication and possible links to more sources, a much larger selection of illustrations can be published and this is to the benefit of the readers. But a balance should be kept and image overloading should be avoided. However, regardless of whether the publication is in print or electronic, the reader will be deprived of the sensation of the original illustration and will not be aware of the selection process. On the other hand, the reader will enjoy an attractive book with a content that is logically presented. With many editions, it is the choice of illustrations that ultimately determines in the final appearance of the book. In addition to the image selection, their placement in the context, the sequence, the format, and the reproduction technique are also very important.

It is the editor's responsibility to decide, along with the graphic editor, which illustrations are to be used and which sources will provide them. Usually, when the planning of a publication starts, a vision of the illustrative approach is already created. Our practical advice is to start creating a list of potential illustrations as soon as possible. Every illustration should be labelled, and should have a credit line (source line) and the expected price. The prices of illustrations vary, based on different book trade markets, and greatly depend on the type of illustration and the effort needed to produce it. A book on a contemporary sculptor, painter or architect will be very demanding and time-consuming for a photographer who is to provide images for it. Also, a skilled photographer will have to be hired in order to have high-quality images. As many professionals in publishing, photographers specialise and it is not difficult to find out who specialises in what type of photography. If, on the other hand, reproductions of original documents are needed, the best quality is achieved by scanning them in the graphic studio. If documents are of high value they will have to be insured before they are taken out of a library. It is best to accompany them to the studio and never leave them unattended. Regardless of the origin of the illustrations, their source should always be stated in the text and in the imprint. This requirement will generally be stated in the copyright agreement.

But back to the list of illustrations. For practical reasons, if a publication is to have both black and white and colour illustrations, it is good to make two separate lists. After the wishlist of illustrations is completed, the search can start. This task should be assigned to a person who is well acquainted with the collections of memory institutions and is familiar with the private collectors of items related to the content of the future publication. Often this search is done by the author or the editor of the publication. The easiest solution for the publisher is when the author can supply images of good quality and known source, since he or she knows the content and is connected to the intellectual environment. Digital archives of illustrations are often used in commercial publishing, but most libraries will not need these kinds of sources, since they mostly publish in cultural and scientific fields. In the search for illustrations one must be mindful of the content and the quality of images. If an image is of low quality, the quality of its reproduction will be even lower or it will demand a lot of touching up to bring it to an acceptable level.

Once the illustration is located, if it is copyrighted a contract with the owner needs be signed to secure its publication. Many publishers owe their success and reputation to the work of their graphic editors. Considering that many readers decide to borrow or buy a book depending on its graphic appearance, the importance of a graphic editor is apparent.

Special attention is paid to the cover design. If a book is to be part of an already existing series, the designer will have to apply the existing technical features. By the same token, if a book is a separate publication the designer will start from scratch and do their best original work to make an attractive cover. Cover design is very important to every publisher because it is the reader's first interaction with the publication.

Before a publisher decides on a cover, a graphic editor will make several suggestions for editors or the editorial board to discuss. To bring in fresh ideas and have provocative solutions, publishers may decide to outsource the design of a cover, either printed or electronic. Perhaps it is even more difficult to design a cover for electronic books considering a digital surrounding in which a future reader makes a decision among millions of choices. There is a difference in choosing a book from a bookshop window and from a web page.

Before submitting the final version of the cover design, the graphic editor will design a few versions of it for the editorial board or the editor to discuss. Based on this discussion a final decision will be made. Often an artist such as a photographer, painter or an illustrator is hired to work on the cover design. Such an artist can take over designing a cover or a dust jacket, or they can make a photograph, painting or a drawing that can be used as a base for the graphic editor on which to base the final design. Graphic editors will often choose an existing work of art to be used in the cover design. It is the publisher's responsibility to arrange for permissions for a graphic designer to use such artwork.

Aside from being appealing to the eye, the book cover must display the basic information about the publication: author's name, title of the work, subtitle and the publisher's logo. The graphic editor must design preliminary pages including the copyright page. An important part of graphic design is the choice of a typeface. Graphic designers of today have a vast choice of typefaces with many variations, while in the time of letterpresses, up until the 1970s, they had to use what was available in the print shop. Sometimes print shops were chosen based on the choice of typefaces they offered, although a basic selection was usually available.

In determining the graphic characteristics of print type, apart from choosing a typeface, the graphic editor decides on the width of the column, font size, letter spacing and line spacing. Typeface and font size must be specified for titles, subtitles, notes and indexes.

Paper selection is often done by a graphic editor as well. Here a graphic editor must consult with the editor in charge because the price of the paper will significantly affect the final price (but also the look) of the publication.

After reading a manuscript, the first thing a graphic editor considers is the format of the publication. Most of the time a graphic editor is limited by standard paper formats. With the choice of a format begins the story of book production. If the manuscript is part of a series, the format of the publication is already decided. However, each series has to have started at one time. That point determined its fate and lifespan.

A book is for reading. This might be an imperative that should be imposed on every graphic editor. It can be said that there are two kinds of graphic editors: those who know how to find a balance between the reader's needs and their own professional ambitions, and those who superimpose their professional ambitions onto the needs of readers. Also, there are graphic designers who read the manuscript and those who do not. Every publisher highly regards the work of a graphic editor because it establishes the first contact with a potential customer or reader. A graphic editor builds the physiognomy of a publishing house. Almost all publishing houses have a recognisable visual identity, thanks to the efforts of a graphic editor. Graphic editing is certainly a profession that is both an art and an application, and there are not many professions where the author awaits the result of their work with so much uncertainty and anticipation as a graphic editor awaits the first print.

Therefore, a graphic editor who has read a manuscript carefully has no lesser role in publishing than the author or the editor of the publication. Parts of the process in making a layout is truly teamwork; however, the finishing touches are in the graphic editor's control. When less demanding publications are made, the graphic editor can decide on the basic technical characteristics of a publication and hand it over to a technical editor to finish it by following their strict instructions.

Rewriter

There is a fine line that distinguishes the editor's tasks from those of a sub-editor or rewriter. The rewriting can be done by the editor and the task consists of a meaningful composition of an existing manuscript. The rewriting is also necessary when publishing collected papers, where manuscripts from different authors are published in one volume. The rewriting might refer to writing of titles and subtitles, the structure and the length of manuscripts, style of citing or avoiding repeating the same content.

Sometimes rewriting is necessary in a work of a single author. The arrangement of the content might be redistributed according to the taste of the potential reader, as it is an editor's job to know its readers' likes and dislikes. A conscientious editor is a very careful reader of a manuscript. The author who gets a chance to cooperate with such an editor can learn a lot. Editing is a creative craft and much is learned by experience and by collaboration with others. Experienced editors have read thousands of manuscripts and they can quickly decide on how to approach it, mainly because they already know the context into which a new publication will fit. So this is another advantage of a library being a publisher, as librarians know the books that have already been published and they can make a fairly good judgement on the context of a new publication in relation to others of similar content. For example, if a biography of a famous person brings new, unknown facts and if it is well designed, it will attract the attention of prospective readers.

A rewriter can make many useful suggestions to a writer. He or she can suggest which parts of the manuscript to expand on or shorten, or advise on the selection of illustrations. Regardless of the desire of every author to be independent, publishers have their specific style, so the library as publisher will also over time build its style and the authors will have to abide by it.

Reviewer

One of the first things an expert on the subject of the book does after picking it up for the first time is to look at the names of reviewers. The practice of listing the names of reviewers differs from publisher to publisher and from country to country, but somehow an experienced reader will know by the type of book if it has been reviewed or not. The reviewing process is an imperative in scholarly publications but it is also desirable in other types of publication. This is especially so when libraries are publishing because they might not have a professional on their team who is able to provide a high-quality manuscript. There might be other reasons for reviewing a manuscript. Paradoxically, a wish to reject a manuscript might also be a reason, but with library publications this will rarely be the case because they are most often the ones commissioning the manuscript. Even when a publisher is convinced that a manuscript is worthy of publishing, it is advisable to get confirmation from one or two experts. Many publishers, libraries especially, will look for financial subsidies to help with publishing expenses. Reviews are usually a requirement for such applications, and the reviews have to be written by experts in the field. Many publishers have a number of associates with whom they discuss various topics related to work, where opinions on the key points of the profession are shaped and where the quality of writing or manuscripts is discussed. These discussions are valuable for choosing a reviewer.

Translator

Publications in a foreign language are an endless source of inspiration for publishers and libraries. Publishing a translation is a challenging job. A publisher's reputation can be evaluated through the translations it publishes. The reading public will judge and rate the publisher based on the choice of titles, quality of translation, context in which the translation is published, etc. To someone outside the profession it might seem that publishing a translation is as simple (or as complex) as that of any other manuscript. You buy the rights, hire a translator and when the translation is finished you proceed as with all other manuscripts. But, as for every other publication, a translation needs a context too. A publisher who is creating its profile and a reputation in the book trade will use translations to fill gaps in the thematic field and publish works that do not exist in the native language. Libraries as publishers rarely publish translations, so it might seem that the issue of translation does not apply to them. That, however, is not the case. Take, for example, the proceedings of academic and professional conferences where invited speakers, often from various countries, submit their work in their native tongue. In such cases translation is not needed for the whole publication but only for specific parts.

There are big differences between publishing fields, and the incentive to publish a translation of non-fiction and fiction will differ. In the case of translating non-fiction, the publisher will pay attention to the development of the terminology in the national language, being aware that the advancement of science and culture depends on it. So, from the choice of the title that is going to be translated to the choice of a translator, publishing of translations is a complex task. The translator must not only know the language but must be acquainted with the subject field of the text to be translated. Translations are often published on subjects of which terminology has not yet been adopted into the national language. Such situations require collaboration with experts from different fields and extensive synchronisation of the terminology. The publisher is often aware that translation solutions are less than ideal and tries everything to make them as good as possible, but then might publish less-than-ideal solutions because it is the only way to bring about terms that will be widely accepted. Precisely because of the use of specific technical terminology, it is necessary that an expert on the subject who is also a native speaker of the particular language checks the text after it has been translated.

Language (copy) editor

Every editor tries to perfect all professional aspects of the publication and the language is certainly one of the principal indicators of quality. That is why there is a language editor. Many publishers, including libraries as publishers, will outsource the task of a language editor. One of the main reasons for this is that in the organisational chart of a library, it will be difficult to find a staff member who can do both language editing and their regular work. Besides, language editing might be an occasional project which at times will require editing numerous manuscripts in a short time. By outsourcing, the library as publisher can assign manuscripts to different language editors and this way have a number of manuscripts edited in the required time.

The main responsibility of a language editor is to make sure that the manuscript complies with the language standards and terminology, but the corrections must be approved by the author. If the author approves the corrections the manuscript can continue its journey through the publishing house. If the publisher is working with a particular language editor for the first time, it might be a good idea to ask for a sample of language editing work on 10 or 20 pages and have the author approve it. If the approval by the author is done at the end of the process instead, and if the author does not accept the corrections, the language editing effort is wasted. A publisher might encounter authors who think their work needs no language editing. In such cases the publisher needs to take a look at the manuscript and decide whether that is the case. The publisher might honour the author's wish but with stipulation that in the book it reads that the language editing is done by the author, or the publisher might refuse such a request. It is our advice to edit the language of every manuscript that a library is going to publish and to outsource that task to experienced language editors who are knowledgeable in the subject field of the manuscript.

Many language editors are proofreaders as well. It is practical for a library to have a language editor also to do proofreading for quality and financial reasons. When a language editor does both, the advantage is that they are already familiar with the manuscript and will do a better job proofreading it. Also, it might be financially beneficial for the publisher to have one person do two tasks as the honorarium in such a case might be somewhat smaller than if the work was done by two different people.

Proofreader

During the publishing process all sorts of errors may occur – in typing, numeration, layout, etc. Remember, errors are noticed only when the book is printed. In online electronic publications it is very easy to correct a typo. But how can an offline or hybrid electronic publication be corrected? Or worse yet, a printed one? To correct a mistake a publisher should go from one customer to the other and make corrections in copies they bought, or correct all the copies still in stock. Have you ever seen an *errata corrige* leaflet in a book you bought? Not in a long time, or never? This is what publishers had to do in order to correct the errors in books that were already printed because the proofreading was not done properly. Proofreading is an old profession. The proofreader looks for and corrects the typos. In the hierarchy of editing responsibilities, proofreaders are at the bottom of the ladder but their work is very important for the final look of the publication. Proofreading started in the time of codices. In those ancient times scribes and scriptoriums competed on who could make fewer errors. It was a matter of professional dignity to have as few errors as possible. Scriptoriums would award a prize to a customer who would find an error in their codex. Even if those times are long gone, it is still embarrassing for publishers if errors occur. It is simple to avoid this. There is a need for a dedicated person to read the layout before it is published. Several readings are necessary, but usually three will do. And the print dummy must also be checked! One should not read it off the screen. For some reason it is much easier to skip an error on a screen. One will not regret the time and money spent on proofreading because the publication will be accurate and worthy of pride. In certain demanding publications, such as encyclopaedias, dictionaries and lexicons, proofreading is done by three different proofreaders in order to reduce the possibility of an error to a minimum.

Although the proofreader's job is almost mechanical, they often discover not only typos but also errors in the content. Proofing is often done by a language editor but in large publishing houses the proofreader's job is a separate, full-time position.

Designer

People like to talk about medical problems – the wrong diagnosis that was given to them, the wrong drugs prescribed, the mistakes made by medical doctors. Laypeople often have opinions and think they have the knowledge that took the actual experts years of study and experience to acquire. This behaviour can be called ignorance. The same goes for design. With the advent of computers, many people who acquired this wonderful machine thought that it was all they needed to become a designer. It is very difficult to get an unformatted, plain text from a writer. Ask for it and see what you get. The title will be bold, the subtitles will be in italics, etc. Yes, it is nice to experiment with fonts for fun, but when one thinks of being a designer only because one has a computer at hand, and librarians often do, then the outcome is no longer so funny. Perhaps a designer will not immediately understand what the publisher wants. Designing is merely a technical job. The designer must study the manuscript in order to not only understand the content but also to be able to anticipate the reading audience's taste. For this reason it is important to give the designers as much information as possible and explain what is expected of them. A good designer will offer several prototypes, and after choosing one the publisher should give the designer carte blanche. It is important to clarify the difference between a graphic editor and a designer. In the print environment the graphic editor is also a designer, specifying all the visual and technical characteristics of the publication. In the electronic environment, a designer is also a graphic editor who visually shapes the content and its graphic characteristics, primarily meaning layout design and typeface selection. To put it concisely: the graphic editor establishes the visual and technical characteristics of a publication and this is a major role in a print publishing environment.

Design is a newer profession, but it is a dominant one in the electronic environment. Because of the opportunities provided by new technologies, this profession took over the graphic editor's task of establishing the technical characteristics of the publication. In the print environment, what nowadays is done by a designer used to be done by an artist brought in by a publisher when they wanted to additionally equip a publication, and this primarily means the look and design of the book cover.

Statement of responsibility

When customers see a book for the first time, they are either attracted by its look or not, especially if they are buying it as a present. If they are buying a book to study from or for work, its look is less important. However, there is a part of each book that has nothing to do with its appearance and that is the statement of responsibility. Every book has to have a set of data that guarantees its origin. Publishing is a cultural and financial venture, but also a legal one. In legal terms, this means that the content of the publication must be authentic in the sense that the author – the individual or corporate author – is known and that the publisher is legally entitled to bring this content to the audience. Apart from the legal aspects, these data are crucial to libraries because it is the library's job to ensure the identification and retrieval of every publication. For centuries libraries have built the main instruments of library infrastructure – catalogues, bibliographies and databases – based on these data. These instruments are the main link libraries provide to their users so that they can identify and use the content of libraries' collections. From readers' standpoint, the statement of responsibility will have an importance because every responsible reader will want to know what they bought or are reading. In that respect a publication does not differ from any other item of purchase, where we expect to see a trademark and where we wish to acquire an established brand name as a guarantee of quality. From the author's standpoint, the statement of responsibility is important for ensuring their moral and material rights, including the right to publish and to financial compensation not only from a publisher but also from collecting societies that in order to fulfil their financial obligations towards authors collect the usage data from libraries as well. In scholarly publishing, these data are essential for researchers and professors as one of the major indicators of their research projects.

Preliminaries

The sequence and comprehensiveness of a statement of responsibility change from publisher to publisher and from country to country, but once the placement and the sequence are determined publishers try to stay consistent in all their editions. Although there is no set order in which responsibilities must be stated, certain information is expected. One of the possible arrangements is that the title and author/s are listed on page 1, sometimes along with the publisher's name and logo. Commonly found on page 2 is copyright information, cataloguing-in-publication and names of the sponsors who helped with funding. This page also often includes illustration sources and names of the editorial board members. Page 3 is usually a title page, at the bottom of which the place and date of issue are often listed. Finally, there is a set of information that publishers place sometimes in the preliminaries and sometimes at the end of the publication (colophon). This set of data is called imprint and listed there are usually the names of persons responsible for publishing the issue, often including their home towns. Also listed must be the publisher's name, the name of the person legally responsible for the publisher, names of the editors, proofreaders, translators, graphic editor and photographer. Sometimes the names of the reviewers are listed. Also stated are the name and address of the printer, and sometimes the name of the typeface and the paper type.

Scenario 2: A university library in a city of rich cultural heritage has decided to exhibit ancient books from its collection of old and rare books to mark an anniversary of the publication of the first incunabula in the national language and script. The curator of the collection suggested this exhibition to the library management and the management liked the idea. The proposal was adopted a year before the exhibition was to open. While deciding to adopt the proposal to have the exhibition, it was also decided to publish an accompanying catalogue with an introduction from the library manager, text by the collection curator on the basic characteristics of the collection, and images of the exhibited book covers. Under the image of each cover in accordance with cataloguing rules there will be the basic information on each exhibited book as well as additional information on content and the physical condition of each book.

After making these decisions, there were a few more decisions that needed to be made in order to organise a successful exhibition and publish the catalogue on time. This project encompasses two separate activities: an exhibition and a publishing venture – issuing the catalogue. It was necessary to establish a programme committee (for

(Cont'd)

---

the exhibition) and an editorial board (for the publication). Certain things can be done by the same person, although it is advisable to have someone on the editorial board that is familiar with publishing in order for the board to monitor the publishing aspect (publishing plan, particular responsibilities, etc.). The programme committee should – apart from the library manager – include university professors and publishers who deal with historical heritage.

Here is what decisions had to be made and how the project was implemented:

EXHIBITION

- How many books will be exhibited?

    - It was decided to exhibit 50 to 79 books. This number was not too big or too small and the occasion was such that most representative pieces should be shown. The books were to be chosen by their subject and each subject was to be equally represented: religion, astronomy, philosophy, history, medicine, etc.

- How will the books be exhibited?

    - The books will be exhibited in horizontal glass cases underneath protective glass. The most interesting reprints of images from the books will be displayed on the walls above the cases. Next to each book and each reprint will be a description that will also be used in the catalogue.

- Who will select which books will be shown in the exhibition?

    - Aside from the curator, selection will be done by an associate with the following background: an expert on medieval history specialising in local history, author and editor of numerous scholarly papers and books on the history of the city where the library is located, with extensive experience in setting up historical exhibitions, expert in ancient Greek and Latin and a

(Cont'd)

regular library patron. If such a person cannot be found, several people are to be appointed.

- Who will be responsible for the exhibition as a whole?
  - The library manager will be responsible for the entire project, especially for the finances.
  - The organisational team will consist of the manager, the curator, the bookbinder and the associate.
- Who will be responsible for publishing the catalogue?
  - The library manager.
- Where will the exhibition be located?
  - It was decided to host the exhibition in a public space, close to but not in the library. The library has an exhibition space but hosting the exhibition in an even more public space will attract more visitors who are not necessarily affiliated with the university. It was thought that this will have a better marketing effect.
- Who will collect the addresses for the invitations?
  - The library address book for similar occasions will be used.
- Opening time and date
  - The exact date of the publishing of the incunabula, in the evening hours.
- How long will the exhibition be on show?
  - One month.

Below is the list and descriptions of the decision concerning the publication of catalogues.

PUBLISHING – CATALOGUE, POSTER, INVITATIONS

Aside from the decisions made in the first phase, the following needs to be decided:

- **When will the catalogue be presented to the public?** At the opening night.

(Cont'd)

- **Will the catalogue be given for free or will it be for sale?** It will be handed out free of charge at the opening night. Later it will be for sale but at a very affordable price. It will be given to journalists for free.

- **Is it necessary to hire a professional to edit the content page of the catalogue?** The associate in charge of book selection will be in charge of editing the catalogue.

- **How long will the introductory text be?** Between three and five pages of text.

- **Is it imperative that the catalogue is a standard size?** No, but the invitation has to be a standard size and the poster must be 50cm × 70cm.

- **Who will do the design and graphic editing?** Associate, local freelance professional who is well known for their work on graphic design of historical publications.

- **Who will print the catalogue?** Several local printing houses will be contacted and the best offer will be accepted; at least three offers will be considered.

- **Will the print be monochromatic or in colour?** The print will be monochromatic, in the colour chosen by the graphic editor. The main reason for this decision was the fact that the covers of the exhibited books are also monochromatic.

- **How many catalogues will be printed?** For example, if the difference in price between 300 and 500 catalogues is not too big, 500 will be printed. The print run has to be estimated on a case-by-case basis as it always depends on the estimated number of users – invited guests, future users and institutions that might be interested in including the catalogue in their collection.

- **Who will ensure the funding and oversee the spending?** The library manager.

All of the tasks were completed according to the plan. The catalogues, the posters and the invitations were printed on time, the exhibition was well attended and special effort

(Cont'd)

was put into communication with schools so that as many students as possible could visit the exhibition. It turned out that the decision to host the exhibition in a public space was a good one and that the design of the exhibition was well coordinated with the design of the invitations, the poster and the catalogues. This was because of the input from not only the library manager and the collection curator but also from the programme board and the editorial board.

The editorial board decided on the editor, created the publishing plan, monitored the deadlines to keep them in accordance with the plan, advised in cases of doubt, and some members were personally involved in editing.

The editor worked on collecting the introductory text and made sure that the book descriptions were correct and finished on time. After he collected the introductory text, he passed them to the editor, and after they were edited he gave them to the graphic editor.

After receiving the manuscript (introductory texts and book illustration captions), the graphic editor made a prototype of the catalogue and gave it to the editor for approval. Once he got the approval, he sent the catalogue to the printing house that the library chose as the best.

The library manager made sure the spending was according to the financial plan. Prior to approval for publishing the catalogue, she secured funding from the city government. The city government is also a partial supporter of the library; they are responsible for funding the preserving and completing the collection of old and rare books.

Final notes on basic professions in library publishing

The aim of Chapter 6 is to make librarians aware of the complexity of publishing production as to the variety of professions that are involved. Different professional tasks are described to help the reader follow all the necessary steps needed to produce a quality publication. This does not mean that all of the tasks described have to be outsourced. The intention is to suggest that all of these steps have to be carried out with dedication and in a set sequence. For example, it is wrong to start a publishing process before the financial plan is completed, do the language editing before a reviewing process is finished, or commission the layout before the language editing is done.

Skipping steps will not save time, as the time will have to be spent doing it again. If a publishing process is not well managed, it becomes not only more time-consuming but can also fail, despite the contributions from all the experts.

Note

1. Courtesy of Zoran Velagić, Associate Professor at The Josip Juraj Strossmayer Univeristy, Osijek, Croatia (*zvelagic@ffos.hr*); translated from Croatian by the authors.

7

Variety in library publishing

Abstract: This chapter describes different types of library publishing. First, different types of libraries are described, and then publishing is explained through the basic grouping of libraries into national, research and university, special, school and public. Some examples of library associations as publishers are also given. Major kinds of print and electronic publications are listed in respect to this grouping with emphasis on the role of university and research libraries because of the very dynamic changes that have taken place within this group of libraries since the 1980s. Digital libraries are described as a special kind of library because they are a publishing project in themselves.

Keywords: digital libraries, national library publishing, research and university library publishing, special library publishing, school library publishing, public library publishing

Library types

Grouping of libraries is different in different countries. Even the large world organisations such as UNESCO (United Nations Educational, Scientific and Cultural Organization) and IFLA (International Federation of Library Associations and Institutions) group libraries differently. UNESCO classifies libraries in six major categories: national libraries,

libraries of institutions of higher education, other special non-specialised libraries (may fulfil the functions of a national library for a specified geographic area), school, special (such as parliament, associations, research institution other than university, institute, business, firm, etc.), and public libraries (Recommendation concerning the International Standardization of Library Statistics, 1970: 145). Under the entry 'Activities and Groups (Division of Library Types)' on the IFLA website[1] sections are listed dealing with different types of library. Some are classified by the criteria of the subject area (e.g. law libraries, art libraries, social science libraries, etc.), and some according to the type of the parent institution to which the library belongs or audience it serves (e.g. academic and research libraries, national libraries, public libraries, etc.). Therefore, groupings overlap so one library may at the same time be a part of the 'academic and research libraries' group but also in the 'law libraries' group.

Other ways to classify libraries exist. They are all results of historical factors, interaction among libraries and user groups or decisions by the organisation classifying them. Often different library types with different functions carry the same category name, and sometimes the same tasks are common to different library types. Therefore, as is often the case with classifications, they are relative, as is the classification used in this book. For the purposes of this book, which deals with libraries as publishers, libraries are grouped by characteristics of their roles as publishers into five categories: national libraries, research and university libraries, special libraries, school libraries and public libraries. When it comes to publishing in libraries, it has already been mentioned that libraries have always published, and that they differ according to their type of publication. Naturally this depends on their specific mission statements, reader groups, library collections and their public role. There is one more type of library that ought to be mentioned in the context of library publishing, even though it is beyond the scope of these classifications, and that is the digital library. The digital library is a special type of library that can serve as part of any of the aforementioned types of library, yet can be a stand-alone library.

Librarians participate in creating publishing products in:

- national libraries
- research and university libraries
- special libraries
- school libraries
- public libraries
- library associations.

Librarians also participate in the creation of digital libraries through special publishing projects.

Digital libraries

Nowadays it is difficult to grasp what all is assumed by the term digital library. This also raises the question as to why a collection of digital documents is called a digital library. And what is the term global digital library supposed to mean? What is the relationship between the traditional paper library, a hybrid library containing both printed and digital documents as well as services, and digital libraries? What is the difference between a digital collection and a digital library? In order to make their collections available to as many users as possible, all libraries nowadays are present in the digital environment; however, that does not make them digital libraries. Librarians know how many e-mails they receive a day about yet another conference on digital libraries. A good number of these papers in these conferences try to explain what this term means, as well as its content, its scope and potential impact on readers. To explain today's meaning of the term digital library, volumes more would have to be written in addition to the ones that already exist. For the purposes of this book, we want to emphasise that no matter what kind of digital library is in question, we consider it to be a publication – a collection of electronic publications. Perhaps collections of digital documents got the name *digital library* because their creators wanted to make a systematic, accessible, searchable, user-friendly collection of documents. The creators probably took traditional libraries as a model and by naming the collections digital libraries they wanted to adopt the basic features of libraries. It is not enough to simply create a document and put it on the web. If the document is not searchable, the users who need it, or may need it, will not be able to find it. Therefore the document must be equipped with the complete mechanism that will ensure access to the bibliographic data and the interface that will allow for accessing, searching and viewing. In order to comply with these requirements, librarians had to develop new and improve on old ways of cataloguing, create new standards, learn new computer skills as well as collaborate with computer specialists. In our preparation for the section on digital libraries we mostly rely on the work of Christine Borgman[2] and Tefko Saracevic.[3] Texts written by these two authors shed light on many issues concerning digital libraries and those who wish to further explore this interesting topic will surely benefit from their work.

Digital libraries – apart from being electronic publications – are also a great topic for research. Although it sometimes seems that it is easier to secure funds for building a digital library than for researching it, topics related to digital libraries such as searchability, evaluation, effect they have on reading populations of all ages and categories are steadily gaining the floor on the research scene. Before we get to the following topic of publishing characteristics with regard to library publishing, we felt it necessary to mention digital libraries not only because we think of them as publications but because we also think of them as infrastructure. Perhaps it is too bold to say that digital libraries became the mental infrastructure, but we dare to say that they are the cohesive force that influenced what is known in information science as the convergence of disciplines, convergence of memory institutions and convergence of media. Skill and knowledge of librarianship in document processing evolved into the indispensable innovation in the world of digital libraries and that is the development of information-seeking and retrieval. That is why digital libraries are, as we see them, at the same time a research challenge and a publishing product. A digital library is a publishing venture in itself, but so is every document it contains. It is a separate and, by its nature, new and complex product with an intricate hierarchical structure. Considering the fact that digital libraries contain documents kept on different media, its creation and development require complex editorial involvement. Libraries that store units which combine text, sound, images and motion images must be organised in such a way that it will relate all media in that entity and as such will offer a reader new value that is not possible to achieve in traditional libraries. The clear hierarchical structure offers readers meaningful navigation, both within an individual publication and throughout the whole library. Approaching digital libraries as a publishing product requires fundamental knowledge of culture as well as technological skills. Various products that carry the word *digital* can be found in libraries of all kinds. The issues around the final form of these products must be approached responsibly. Selection of content, its presentation, relevancy, series of technical issues, issues of preservation, copyright, security and long-term sustainability should be considered. Such an approach will ensure achievement of the library's mission and readers' satisfaction, the importance of which we have stressed many times throughout this book.

Digital libraries:

- are publishing ventures in themselves;
- exist in all types of library or as stand-alone libraries;
- are complex publishing products – every document is a publishing product as well as the digital library as a whole;
- are a convergence of memory institutions, information science disciplines and media;
- have multiple functions, wide access and digital preservation.

National libraries

The primary mission of all national libraries is to be the bibliographic centre of the nation that founded it and to collect all that has been published *in* that country and *about* that country (including the publications by the nationals of that country regardless of their residency) anywhere in the world and in any language or medium. This means that every national library is the most complete collection of national interest and as such an inexhaustible source of research material, thus publishing material as well. Each national library is implicitly part of every research that is published with the use of its collections. However, each national library has publishing responsibilities, often regulated by law, that are a result of its mission, which is, among other things, to publish current national bibliographies for books and periodicals, print and electronic. In addition to compiling the current bibliography, many libraries give great attention to retrospective bibliographies and bibliographies of particular collections. National library special collections, such as a graphic collection, allow it to present a part of its wealth to the public. In the case of visual art, virtual and live exhibitions are often organised and usually accompanied by published catalogues describing pieces as well as the authors and time period of the art. National libraries publish information about their institution and activities. Considering that national libraries are prestigious public institutions of a country, it is only natural to report to its taxpayers on their activities through publishing their strategic plans and yearly reports. An example of this is the Library of Congress web page, which shows information on the institution's publishing activities and, in a prominent place, displays its annual report[4] accompanied by other relevant documents – financial statements, budget justifications, etc.[5] Yearly reports of the European national libraries are uniform thanks to cooperation within the Foundation Conference of European National Librarians (CENL). These reports are structured in such a way that their content can be compared with one another. Also, they sometimes contain data on library publishing.[6] The libraries mentioned also have other content on their web pages that shows their publishing activity, for example the British Museum Library:[7]

> The British Museum Library first started publishing in around 1780. The original productions were catalogues of the core collections of the library, a tradition which

has continued until the present day. . . . British Library Publishing was founded in 1981, and has grown substantially since then, both in terms of breadth and number of publications. Our scope has now widened to include the art and history of books and manuscripts, including sacred texts, facsimile editions of valuable texts and general guides to our more famous collection items. We currently publish around 50 books and audio CDs a year.

Aside from publishing reports of their activities, national libraries also issue publications based on their rich collections. Readers especially appreciate guides to the collections. Since national libraries have curators for certain collections, they publish guides founded on in-depth research of not only certain sections of collections but even individual units. In this way national libraries allow users a closer look than they would get by searching a library catalogue.

In this group of publications, an important place is given to guides to libraries and library services. Considering the complexities and wide array of services available, national libraries offer publications such as leaflets and brochures about library services, rights, rules and regulations. Announcements of new services are of great value to library users. Without such published guides, library patrons, both those who are merely visiting and those spending long hours researching, would hardly be able to satisfy their library needs such as usage of rare book and manuscript collections, or printing from microfilms or digital documents that are not available on the web outside the library.

A national library newspaper collection can be of special interest to particular readers (researchers as well as those interested in antiques) and the public. For various reasons that range from the sentimental to the scientific, readers find old newspapers to be very interesting. Libraries that own such collections keep them especially protected and allow only restricted use of these materials. There are two basic ways to allow access to such materials while keeping them protected. One is microfilming and digitalising and the other is reprint publishing. Digitalisation and web access are gaining ground over expensive and complex reprint publishing; however, if the original publication is especially rare, valuable reprints will still be made. Such ventures are particularly valuable to library readers as many library collections are incomplete and one of the main reasons for a library to publish a reprint is to complete a collection of all published volumes.

Many libraries have old newspaper collections; national libraries, however, have an obligation to keep and protect old newspapers in such a way that the materials can be used forever. Here we are not concerned about methods of library materials protection and preservation in general, but only the cases that result in publishing the old newspaper in the form of a reprint or digital document. It almost seems that offering access to as many digitised old newspaper volumes as possible has become a matter of prestige among national libraries. Since old newspapers are the most fragile library units because of the poor quality of the paper on which they are printed, yet are frequently used by the patrons, ensuring digital access is a great contribution to their protection while allowing the maximum number of patrons to read them at the same time.

In the same way that they publish old newspaper reprints, national libraries also publish other materials such as old music sheets, manuscripts, incunabulae, guides and rulebooks for librarians and others. All of this points to the fact that national libraries' holdings are a great resource for their publishing endeavours. National libraries use this great potential in abundance. The introduction of computers to libraries, including the national ones, sparked a series of joint publishing ventures such as Europeana, European Digital Library Project, FUMAGABA project,[8] etc. National library publishing will certainly grow and advance, although in a digital age these libraries face new and unexpected difficulties, such as data harvesting and allowing or restricting access to commercial content. In any event, national libraries face interesting times in terms of collecting, protecting and providing access to library holdings where publishing plays an important role.[9]

In addition to their own publishing ventures, national libraries have one more significant tie to publishing. It is the responsibility of the national library to collaborate with all publishers of the nation as it is the keeper of the legal deposit copies. The national library assigns the CIP (Cataloguing in Publication) and ISBN (International Standard Book Number) number, which is collected by the International ISBN Agency. By the same token, the national library assigns the ISSN (International Standard Serial Number) collected by the ISSN International Center, and ISMN (International Standard Music Number) collected by the ISMN Agency.

National libraries:

- are an inexhaustible source of publishing materials (about the library itself and its holdings);
- have a current national bibliography publishing duty;
- focus on retrospective and special bibliographies;
- produce strategic documents, yearly plans, reports, the library and its community event information publishing;
- undertake joint ventures and co-publishing projects with publishers;
- collaborate with publishers in the capacity of the national centre for CIP, ISBN, ISSN, ISNM as well as the collector and keeper of legal deposit copies.

Research and university libraries

In addition to national libraries, research and university libraries play a significant role in library publishing. Research and university libraries are different in each country. Most often the research library is at the researchers' service, while university libraries serve students. If, however, a library has a dual role as a research and university library, these two functions overlap to serve both groups. Sometimes research libraries are not part of a university but, for instance, are part of a research lab in a science institute. Such libraries can also serve students, especially doctoral students. Regardless of their name, these libraries serve higher education and research and their specific profile is defined by their user population. Just as their basic functions are similar and related, so is their publishing profile. In the past ten years a new publishing model has been developed as a result of radical changes in user needs and habits. The e-shift we described in Chapter 3 has had a major effect on these kinds of libraries. This shift resulted in decreased use of libraries' physical premises and an increased use of electronic resources and new services offered by research and university libraries. Publishing is a big part of libraries' new services. In research conducted in 2008 about the publishing activities of research libraries in the US, Karla L. Hahn found that:

> These libraries are publishing many kinds of works, but the main focus is journals; 88% of publishing libraries reported publishing journals compared to 79% who publish conference papers and proceedings, and 71% who publish monographs. Established journal titles dominate this emerging publishing sector and are the main drivers of service development, although new titles are also being produced. Although the numbers of

titles reported represent a very thin slice of the scholarly publishing pie, the survey respondents work with 265 titles: 131 are established titles, 81 are new titles, and 53 were under development at the time of the survey. On average, these libraries work with 7 or 8 titles with 6 currently available. (Hahn, 2008: 5)

Another feature established by this research is the new model of partnership between libraries and publishers. Co-publishing was and is a very common way to join forces among publishers, but partnering between libraries and publishers as a business model is very recent. This is not a traditional form of co-publishing as in commercial publishing because both the university library and the university press are part of a university and as such their collaboration is logical and necessary. Although it may sound paradoxical, some university publishers that with time gained certain independence because of commercial reasons became officially separated from their founding universities. Thanks to co-publishing and e-shift, they will again start to collaborate with the universities and to partner up formally. Joint publishing projects could be a first step toward such partnering:

> Partnering is a consistent strategy to diversify program support, and libraries report they often work with multiple partners. Publishing services are not usually treated as an isolated operating unit, the way a university press might be. They are typically embedded in an emerging program of related services – digital repository development, digitization programs, copyright management advising, etc. (Hahn, 2008: 6)

This trend of cooperation between university libraries and university presses is especially developed on campuses. Libraries are trying to find a way to confront budget cuts and rising prices of journal subscriptions and monographs, so electronic publishing seems a logical way to deal with this crisis. University presses are part of the same environment. A majority of the presses are independent and are in fact trade publishers, with the advantage of being able to make use of the overall capital of the university, especially its name. But the golden era of printed journals and monographs is long gone, and university presses have to look for new models. It is still uncertain if partnering with research libraries will in the future lead to much closer connections among university presses and universities. Crow writes: 'In many institutions, the library and the press are taking the lead in developing collaborative publishing ventures intended to demonstrate the potential of integrated campus-based publishing strategies' (Crow, 2009: 6).

This, of course, does not mean that university and research libraries do not publish other types of material aside form scholarly publications. As all other libraries, these also publish catalogues, bibliographies, exhibition guides, newspapers, newsletters, tutorials and miscellanea. Including students in the publishing process primarily aids their affirmation and promotes involvement, but it can also be part of their education or current research.

University and research libraries:

- are intended for researchers and students;
- demonstrate co-operation between libraries and university presses;
- publish scholarly publications, journals, catalogues, bibliographies, newsletters, tutorials, etc.;
- create institutional repositories for teaching materials, theses and scholarly publications.

Institutional repositories

In principle, every type of library and each institution can have a repository if it is needed. Thanks to the decreased cost of data storage, repositories are becoming an increasingly acceptable way of storing and publishing materials. Similar to digital libraries, repositories are publishing products. We could actually consider them a form of digital libraries (digital collections, certainly) as they function by similar principles. Perhaps the only difference is in the fact that digital repositories are the result of the efforts of the community that primarily uses them. Similarity between digital repositories and digital libraries is in the fact that they both have many definitions. Basically, repositories are digital document storage that can be used by others as much or as little as the owner or the creator of the documents allows. Lynch states:

> . . . a university-based institutional repository is a set of services that a university offers to the members of its community for the management and dissemination of digital materials created by the institution and its community members. It is most essentially an organizational commitment to the stewardship of these digital materials, including long-term preservation where appropriate, as well as organization of access or distribution. (Lynch, 2003: 2)

Since computer technology allows storage and access to all digital-born and digitised contents, repositories are proven to be an excellent way of storing and providing access to all kinds of digital documents. Considering the nature of their work, it is not surprising that digital repositories are most used by researchers and students. What is most important in this environment is to have the content classified, stored and always available regardless of their e-format.

By considering the basic characteristics of repositories, one can conclude that they are a sort of digital library with accessibility (that at this point we can refer to as a degree of openness to the public) regulated by the document creator or owner. Repositories are like a pantry in a household where food supplies are kept organised and fresh. The host may enter the pantry and choose whatever he wants, but the guests will only be able to use what the host picks out for them. Examples of this are learning tools. A teacher or researcher, being the creator, is the one who decides who will use these tools and to what extent. The same applies to authors who use repositories to store their draft versions.

Institutional repositories are a valid alternative to traditional commercial or institutional publishing. They can also be a way to publish manuscripts that could not find their way into traditional, paper publishing. In addition, teachers and scholars are becoming increasingly aware that they have to change the way they teach the curriculum to the students as well as the way they present their research. So in regard to the knowledge they contain, the function of the repositories can be viewed in two ways – publishing of educational materials and scholarly publishing. All who work with students are aware of the fact that today's students use multimedia intensively and that analogue teaching materials have a lesser role than they did in the past. This obliges teachers to incorporate audio and video materials in their teaching, as well as in the teaching materials. The former formats of printed textbooks are changing and adapting to new teaching requirements where it sometimes seems that the students are the ones who, more than teachers, dictate the rhythm of innovation as they adopt new technologies faster and sometimes even participate in their creation. New technologies allow the possibility of enriching the teaching materials with embedded graphics, audio and video materials, all linked with datasets and applications needed to manipulate data, etc. To fulfil such requirements, investing in hardware and software is necessary. Ithaca Report informs on these issues in detail:

> ...a new generation of devices for consuming information will require that content be organized and presented in new ways.
>
> The librarians consulted for this study were more enthusiastic about the potential of multimedia than other constituents. Provosts tended to be more conservative, associating 'publishing' primarily with books and journals. (Brown et al. 2007: 14)

Since there is a need to publish multimedia teaching materials, and most sources needed for making them can be found in libraries, libraries are the most logical and probably the best location to place materials production labs. Institutional repositories have solved one of the big problems in accessing doctoral theses. Since doctoral dissertations are *grey literature*, the paradox was that access to most recent research was very limited. But, according to McDowell, as Royster reports (2007: 5): 'Publishing doctoral dissertations in an IR is not unusual; in fact, they make up the largest single document type in a recent survey of IRs in the United States.' Naturally, to use such documents one must first have access to them.

> But it is especially worth noting the great difference that is made by making them open-access as opposed to limited-access or subscription-access. The experience at

our IR has shown this difference to be about a 60-fold increase in downloads (and thus in impact) of open-access as opposed to limited access dissertations. (Royster, 2007: 5)

The other important role of institutional repositories must not be overlooked: the role of institutional memory as they serve in digital preservation.

Those who are familiar with new trends in education influenced by new technologies know that students are not only its users but often also the creators. Librarians who work in research libraries are all aware of the upcoming trends in university and research libraries publishing activities, with clear indications that publishing might become one of their primary services.

Naturally this will have an impact on library budgets. However, since the majority of these libraries are a part of research and educational institutions where publishing is a matter of professional survival, their parent institutions might be inclined to consider providing additional sources of funding for library publishing. Perhaps the funds that in the past were used elsewhere will be directed towards library publishing.

This probable scenario might be aided by the dissatisfaction with expensive commercial publishers, especially in regard to scholarly journals. Development of science and education drives the universities to publish ever increasing numbers of electronic journals, and university administration will probably be more likely to opt for non-commercial publishing such as that offered by their libraries. Great potential for library publishing is in library consortia through which certain niche journals can attain greater visibility.

Besides, one must keep in mind that growing competition in the research environment led to the involvement of librarians in research projects. Many research teams in different phases of their research work closely with librarians, making publishing one of the activities where librarians collaborate with researchers and teachers. It has been said many times and in various ways that a library is the heart of a university. It seems that this truth still holds as the libraries collaborate not only with university computer centres and departments but also with university presses and all the researchers involved in the production and dissemination of publications. According to Lynch, '. . . an effective institutional repository of necessity represents collaboration among librarians, information technologists, archives and record managers, faculty, and university administrators and policymakers' (Lynch, 2003: 2). The issue of institutional repositories brings up the question of organisational roles and the responsibilities of all organisational units within a university. Also, there is the issue of the relationship between scholarly communication and scholarly publishing, where Lynch, for example, is of the opinion that scholarly publishing is a lot more than dissemination of materials while the major role of institutional repositories in fact is dissemination (so-called scholarly communication). Lynch also questions the comprehensiveness of repositories because, while they are oriented towards individual disciplines, scholarly enterprise is diverse. Therefore, '. . . the institutional repository is a complement and a supplement, rather than substitute, for traditional scholarly venues' (Lynch, 2003: 5).[10]

Whatever the future of institutional repositories may be, librarians will have an important role in their development as it is their job to make sure that a publication, be it print or electronic, reaches the reader for whom it was created in the first place.

Institutional repositories:

- serve multiple functions – online storage and publishing;
- include educational materials and/or scholarly publications;
- involve a convergence of media;
- have the potential to increase visibility and accessibility of niche and *grey literature*;
- involve the cooperation of librarians, faculties, information technologists, archive managers, university administrators and policymakers.

Concluding this part of the chapter about university and research library publishing, we could say that this type of publishing is a hot topic of many new developments and up-to-date reports on research in this field. There are indications that librarians are playing a leading role in these new developments and there is a lot of room for development of new user services for the members of academia who, in many cases, are authors themselves. From the publishing standpoint, national, academic and research libraries are specific in many ways when compared with other kinds of libraries, as they often have a separate publishing department, which requires excellent coordination and communication. In recent times, these kinds of libraries have increased their electronic publishing production not only because of the availability of new technologies and the possibilities they provide in production and distribution of publications, but also for the nature of information they publish. The field of scientific information is very dynamic and such information changes and can become obsolete rapidly; electronic publishing provides a means to keep the information up to date.

Special libraries

Special libraries differ not only because of the differences in the purpose of their parent institutions, but also in the complexity of the parent institution or company and the public for which they are intended. Hence some are focused on the people of the community assembled to support a cause or an initiative, such as NGO libraries, and some are more similar to research libraries, such as libraries in large companies with research departments. They can also have a dual purpose, such as libraries in hospitals where they serve the medical staff for research and the patients as a public library. Publishing activity of such libraries depends on the readers for whom they publish. In the case of special libraries that are a part of a company that has a research centre, they are more likely to publish research papers from conferences and other publications similar to the ones a research library publishes, maintaining all the characteristics of research library publishing, such as electronic publishing, because it allows for greater relevance and better access to information. In the case of a library that is part of, for example, public organisations, its publishing activities will mostly be focused on materials that promote the organisation's mission in society or the local community (e.g. newsletters, catalogues, etc.).

Special libraries:

- vary in terms of home institution and potential users;
- can be a research library, for example in a company that has a research centre, or a library open to the public with special interests/needs;
- can publish anything from scholarly publications to newsletters, pamphlets, etc.

School libraries

The main purpose of school libraries is to support the teaching process and their readers are students, teachers and parents. According to the IFLA/UNESCO School Library Guidelines (2002: 3), the mission of the school library is to equip '. . . students with lifelong learning skills' and to develop '. . . their imagination, thereby enabling them to live as responsible citizens.' Therefore, regardless of whether the users are students, teachers or parents, school libraries are always oriented towards students and their achievements. Thus the school library's publishing activities are focused on enriching learning resources and informing, or on affirming the work of the students. Such publications may be catalogues, journals, bulletins and newsletters (students are often involved in creating these publications), books about the school or the community that sometimes include the students' and teachers' work, instructions for using the collections and resources, proceedings from various events, posters, exhibition catalogues, educational materials, tutorials, library blogs and information on the library website. As students are often involved in creating such publications, school library publishing has an additional value as part of the educational process, whether it be as part of a particular subject or extracurricular activities and clubs (e.g. journalist club, art club).

School libraries:

- are for students, teachers and parents;
- publish learning sources, various information and student work;

(Cont'd)

- engage in publishing activities as part of the educational process and instruction;
- use publishing as part of students' extracurricular activities.

Public libraries

Public libraries have the widest audience, ranging from small children to senior citizens. Thus the plethora of publications issued by public libraries is the widest and most diverse. It ranges from picture books for preschool children, novels and poems by librarians and by members of the community, and books on local history to scholarly papers and symposia proceedings. Because of such a wide range of publishing subjects, public libraries often need and look for publishing partners. Considering the role public libraries play in any community, there is almost no organisation, association, club or individual who cannot be a publishing partner to a public library. For that reason, the potential public library publishing partner network can be very wide. The situation is similar when it comes to publishing ventures. Public libraries can enter into co-publishing ventures with local government or cultural institutions such as theatres and museums because libraries are cultural institutions and are in some way obliged to contribute to the cultural development of their community. This is especially the case in smaller communities where there are no other cultural institutions. Especially smaller libraries will need partners in order to succeed in publishing ventures and they will most likely outsource certain technical tasks, such as graphic design, most probably printing and very likely the distribution as well.

Publishing in public libraries is often related to other projects or programmes, which implies that the reasons for publishing are often a result of regular library services or some value-added services. For example, as a part of youth services many libraries organise summer reading programmes. Organising such a programme requires marketing in the form of print or electronic publications (posters, brochures, pamphlets, etc.) that will attract the youth to join the programme. Furthermore, offered reading materials should be presented, most often in the form of a bulletin, again in print and/or electronic format, that informs on the content of the books, presents the author, gives recommendations for further reading, and so on. Finally, the project must be documented in order to be evaluated and possibly compared with other such projects. The results of the programme should be presented to other libraries and the public in the form of a report. Such projects will surely result in many publications and the success and visibility of the whole project might just depend on these publications. This is just one example that shows how regular library services generate the need for library publishing activities. The same is true for all services and programmes that are supported by print or electronic materials intended for library users and the whole community.

Public libraries:

- have the widest audience – ranging from small children to senior citizens;
- have librarians as authors;
- are in partnership with the community;
- take part in co-publishing and outsourcing;
- are involved in publishing related to the community, library collections and regular library services.

Library associations as publishers

Librarians not only participate in publishing at their own libraries but also within library associations of which they are members – ranging from local to international. There are also library associations that gather librarians of certain library types. Certainly one of the most prolific publishers among the library associations is the International Federation of Library Associations and Institutions (IFLA). IFLA publishes standards, manifestos, guidelines, statements, reports, journals, newsletters, etc., and does it all in print and/or electronic format.[11] All such publications are the result of librarians' and other information science experts' efforts, often volunteers alongside IFLA staff. Some publications are co-published with a commercial publisher.[12]

National library associations issue various publications, written in a national language and translations (of above-mentioned IFLA publications in particular).[13] Librarians participate in various phases of the publishing process – from writing or obtaining the content, editing and reviewing to making the decisions on cover design. Sometimes these publishing projects are a result of joint efforts by libraries and library associations, and often third parties as well. Librarians are expected to not only have the in-depth background in the issue at hand but to also be familiar with the publishing process of which they are a part.

Library associations' publishing activities are very dynamic and they have always played an important role in the development of their profession. In librarianship these publications are of utmost importance, as certain standards and norms may be used nationally and internationally only after they have been published.

Although library associations could earn substantial amounts of money, they are not commercial publishers. It often happens that the price of a publication only just covers the cost of its making. The purchasing price of such publications is often lower than that of similar publications as the librarians participate in the professional associations and their publishing on a volunteer basis, or as part of their professional obligations. Library associations do not publish for profit but as a professional responsibility; therefore, the profit from publishing ventures is directed towards projects that contribute to the development of librarianship and to new publishing ventures.

Library associations as publishers:

- are international, national and local associations and associations of particular types of libraries;
- publish as a not-for-profit activity;
- publish as a professional responsibility.

Concluding remarks concerning all types of library

Regardless of the library type, in order to create an environment conducive to publishing activities that are to become an integral part of the library as a whole, publishing must be part of a library's strategic plan. Including publishing services into library strategic plans, or rather making library publishing strategic plans, will facilitate long-term and short-term profiled planning and will facilitate decision-making related to thematic range, titles, human and material resources, types of publication, publication format, commercial aspects and possible partnerships. There are many methods by which to complete a strategic plan and various accompanying tools that facilitate its operations, such as manuals and guidelines. Regardless of the methods and accompanying tools, a checklist that examines the current approach to library publishing and establishes new benchmarks for more successful library publishing creativity will always come in handy (see Appendix 1). Using such a checklist can be considered a prerequisite to making a library publishing strategic plan. Appendix 2 gives basic principles as an aid for making such a plan. This is a suggested list and each library should adjust it to its own circumstances, of which a clearer picture will be achieved after completing Appendix 1.

Notes

1. See the list of the sections, available from *http://www.ifla.org/en/library-types* (accessed 12 August 2010).
2. See *http://polaris.gseis.ucla.edu/cborgman/Chriss_Site/Welcome. html (accessed 30 August 2010).*
3. See *http://comminfo.rutgers.edu/~tefko/* (accessed 30 August 2010).
4. Available from: *http://www.loc.gov/loc/pub/* (accessed 30 July 2010).
5. Available from: *http://www.loc.gov/about/reports/* (accessed 30 July 2010).
6. Available from: *http://www.cenl.org/members.php* (accessed 22 August 2010).
7. Available from: *http://publishing.bl.uk/about-british-library-publishing* (accessed 25 December 2009).
8. Available from *http://web3.nlib.ee/cenl/projects.php* (accessed 16 September 2010).
9. Just how extensive national library publishing is in smaller nations is evident from the example of the Croatian National and University Library. This library has a dual function – that of the national as well as of the central university library and this duality is reflected in its publishing. On the library web

pages one can find a link to a library bookstore offering bibliographies, newsletters, library catalogues, art books related to library collections and events held at the library, exhibition catalogues, postcard reprints of units from old and rare book collections, books and electronic publications that are mainly related to cataloguing and primarily intended for librarians. Available from: *http://www.nsk.hr/Info.aspx?id=131* (accessed 15 September 2010).

10. Lynch also discusses the possibility of institutional repositories becoming counterproductive in the future. Available from *http://www.arl.org/resources/pubs/br/br226/br226ir.shtml* (accessed 20 August 2010).

11. A list of publications is available at *http://www.ifla.org/en/ ifla-publications* (accessed 20 August 2010). IFLA Sections are also active in publishing: on the website they provide information about publications developed by the Sections and also publish their newsletters, statements, reports, strategic (action) plans, etc.

12. Currently this is a publishing company from Germany, De Gruyter Saur.

13. For example, the Croatian Library Association (CLA) operates in a country with a relatively small population (approximately 4.5 million), and was founded in 1940. It gathers librarians of 16 regional (county) associations and the so-called CLA Club. Although the CLA as compared with library associations of other countries can be considered small, its publishing production is large. The CLA publishes monographs, professional and scholarly publications of local and foreign authors, library manuals, standards, proceedings from scholarly and professional conferences, guidelines, *Croatian Librarians Herald*, CLA Newsletter, etc. Available from: *http://www.hkdrustvo.hr/hr/izdanja/* (accessed 3 August 2010). In recent years, an increasing number of publications have become available online. All publications are the result of librarians' efforts who are members of the association, and only a small part is outsourced, mainly printing.

8

Relations with other publishers

Abstract: The chapter explains the basics of co-publishing and the formal regulation of relations between co-publishing partners. Advantages of co-publishing are highlighted, as well as the motivation for co-publishing with the aim of bridging the digital divide.

Key words: co-publishing, libraries as co-publishers, digital divide

Co-publishing

Sometimes publishers join forces. The reasons for this might vary, but usually the main reason is to produce a better publication with less money and effort. One publisher might have expert editors on a subject while the other might have interesting material at hand, such as old photographs, old maps, or something else that they alone are not ready or able to publish for some reason. Usually financial reasons are the main obstacle to producing a new publication, but lack of expert personnel can also be a hindrance. If one author is not ready to publish a work independently, authors are often the ones who put two or more publishers in contact with each other. After the agreement is reached, usually a co-publishing contract is signed, specifying who is in charge of what, which resources will be used and who will provide them. If the financial input is to be unequal, the value of other contributions is weighted. At any rate, the budget must be part of the co-publishing agreement, stating who is investing what, and how the profit is going to be divided. Sometimes publishers split the print run proportionally to their investment and organise sales individually, or they hire a distributor and divide the profit from the sales.

There are many benefits of co-publishing. Sharing the investment is surely one of the more important ones. Joining editorial forces can enhance the expertise on the publishing project. Joint marketing can also be advantageous in a similar way. As far as readers are concerned, they might consider the relevance of the publication to be stronger if it has been co-published.

Co-publishing could also be disadvantageous. Problems can arise from disagreements between editors from two or more different publishers. Editors tend to be very creative and sometimes it might be difficult for two or more to harmonise their opinions. Therefore it is always a good solution to put one person in charge of a task.

Libraries as partners in co-publishing

For a library it might be very productive to join forces with professional publishers. In such arrangements, the library is usually the content provider and the publisher does all of the editing and layout. Financial arrangements for such publications can vary, but both partners should agree on the balance of interests. In such co-publishing arrangements, the library (or a library association) has delegated a demanding job to professionals, and a publisher has published another publication and gained additional respect by working with a non-profit organisation.

Co-publishing between libraries and publishers can be driven by different reasons. For a library, this is a way to better accomplish its mission. For a publisher, co-publishing with a library will result in accruing additional intellectual capital, which can be a very strong motivation for this kind of partnership. An important issue with equal access to information is the matter of digital divide. It can, however, be resolved through partnership. In overcoming the problem of digital divide, libraries can partner up with companies, particularly ones in the ICT sector. Also, partnering up with publishers can be especially useful since through joint publishing projects libraries can include the publishers in projects on overcoming the digital divide.

Many pages have been written and talks delivered about the digital divide. The digital divide was identified and became a subject of research with the advent of the digital age and the shift from divided continents to divided groups of society within the same country or the same community. But, the divide is not only concerned with access to technology. In a way, the (information) divide existed even earlier for reasons of unevenly developed library infrastructure and library network. Therefore, some society groups have always been privileged in the sense of access to information over some other groups of society, especially the ones in rural areas or underprivileged metropolitan areas. So the digital divide is not only concerned with access to technology; it also concerns access to the carrier of content, regardless of the kind of technology. This divide is more visible today because the amount of diversified content is growing. With the growing amount of content and increasingly sophisticated search options, the differentiation of users is growing, so today we have new forms of digital divide that concern different kinds of illiteracy. Nevertheless, libraries and publishers long ago provided the answer to this differentiation.

There is no library that can serve all users. There is a library to serve a nation, and there are different types of library to serve different user populations, as mentioned in previous chapters of this book. Publishers specialise in a similar way and as with libraries, the specialisations are fairly intricate. Libraries have a vast experience in finding just the right way to serve different types of reader. So nowadays, when one thinks about new library publishing products, a library as a whole should be considered and its products easily accessible through the web. Overcoming the digital divide can be a strong motivational factor for forming library and publisher associations and at the same time can be a solid ground for raising funds. There is a convergence among libraries, archives and museums that are stimulated by new technologies, and in turn new technologies stimulate cooperation between libraries and publishers in overcoming the digital divide, because with well-thought-out division of labour they can more effectively ensure access to printed or electronic material, each in their own area of expertise.

We are convinced that the traditional professions of publishing and librarianship can give excellent models to follow in the new technology environment. Perhaps not in a practical way, but in the sense of the approach. And this approach is oriented to users' needs.

9

Conclusions

Here we are at the end of our book. We hope that it will inspire you to venture into publishing projects at your library. And for those who are already publishing, we hope you will find this book to be a help with organising this demanding task. We also hope that LIS students who are just preparing to step into the world of library practice will discover through this book just how challenging, inventive and interesting a librarian's job can be. Of course, in order for libraries to be such a place of work, librarians need competencies in the field of publishing. All procedures and scenarios that are described in this book are based on many years of experience working in publishing, libraries and in library and reading associations. Naturally, readings that are listed in the bibliography were a great help in focusing on certain subjects, and for testing our theories and views.

We tried to concisely describe how to approach publishing within library services, from recognising prospective readers' needs, selection of the right subject, and the decision on which medium to publish in and choosing an author, to required competencies and backgrounds of all involved in the publishing process. In this book we have listed all skills expected from a professional publisher as well as overall organisation of the publishing business. And we stress again: do not skip over any part of the sequence of the publishing process; this will save time and money and will result in a quality product.

As was shown in the examples, where library publishing projects are concerned, there seems to be an indispensable approach in deciding whether to publish, why and what. It is the answer to the question: is the publishing project in accordance with the library's mission statement and the needs of the readers? If the answer to this question is in the affirmative, then the decision to publish is the right one because this is the guarantee that the readers' needs will be met.

In all library services, the collections are a foundation for everything. Here we mean not only physical book or electronic collections, but also the context that surrounds the collections, especially the accumulated librarians' knowledge about the collections and needs of their readers. It is for this reason that library publishing based on the collections and professional/academic library services is the most widespread, for example, catalogues, bibliographies, monographs, scholarly papers, conference proceedings, educational materials, etc.

It is well known that libraries are esteemed information institutions. In order to have such a status they have to primarily have information about themselves. Such information must be current, complete, correct and accessible. That is why libraries publish reports, strategic and action plans, reviews of research, examples of good practice, etc. This group of publications certainly includes publications that serve the promotion of libraries in public. Creating a public image of a library aims to spread and confirm the idea of social responsibility that libraries represent. This idea is important for both current and future library readers. Is there a more constructive way to attract new readers than current readers' satisfaction and a positive public image? A publishing service with the purpose of communication with the readers and the public must be done highly professionally as it is one of the liveliest aspects of communication between a library and its readers; this includes invitations and announcements of library happenings. These publishing products can be printed and electronic, but they have to be creative and attractive in order to serve their purpose.

And last but not least, the electronic environment has brought to libraries a whole new and productive perspective on publishing on a previously unimaginable scale. Different libraries use these new opportunities differently. The ways we listed in this book are merely examples of the possibilities, but these possibilities will surely grow and libraries will use them, alone or in cooperation with publishers. All that was said pertains to all kinds of libraries, but electronic publishing is most vigorous in academic libraries because they are the institutions where publishing of scholarly papers is one of the primary activities.

At any rate, after a rough start as far as libraries are concerned, the digital age has proved again that libraries are ingenious institutions. Such ingenuity is demonstrated in their flexibility, multifunctionality, and nowadays not only openness to new technology, but active creation of information and formation of communication technologies to meet customer needs. The tremendous potential of libraries is a result of capital that emerged from the fact that a library is at the centre of the communication between content and a reader. New trends indicate that this status is permanent and it continues to strengthen. Librarians are there to shape it in accordance with the fundamental principles of their profession.

Appendix 1
Checklist for library strategic plan development

How have things been done in the past (elements for evaluation and self-assessment)?

1. Are publishing activities a part of the current library strategic plan? Are they articulated in the mission statement?

2. What is the management's overall attitude towards library publishing?

3. Does the library have a publishing tradition and, if so, what are the main characteristics of this tradition?

4. What was the principal reason for publishing certain publications?

5. How do library publishing activities compare with library publishing activities in the closer or wider community?

6. How many titles has the library published so far?

7. How many planned but not published titles have there been, and why have they not been published?

8. What kinds of publications have been published, how many titles of each kind and in which time periods?

9. What is the ratio between published print and electronic titles?

10. Did the library publish entirely in-house or did it outsource?

11. What was done in-house and what was outsourced?

12. Did the library co-publish any titles? If so, which titles, and what were the experiences from the partnership?

13. What profile of library staff has been involved in publishing ventures and in what publishing tasks?

14. What publishing processes were most often outsourced?

15. What sources of funding were used for publishing projects?

16. What was the main source of funding, and what were the percentages of funding from the smaller donators?

17. Did the publishing ventures result in financial gain and where was it invested?

18. In what way did the library notify the public about its publications (catalogues, web alerts, e-mail alerts, newsletters . . .)?

19. What was the most efficient method?

20. How was the distribution organised?

21. What was the most efficient form of distribution (in terms of number of copies given or sold, or the number of downloads)?

22. What are the positive and negative experiences with in-house distribution as compared with outsourcing?

23. What impact and in which media has publishing production had so far?

24. What is the audience feedback and how was it collected?

25. Is there a current and publicly accessible exact description of tasks related to publishing, ranging from obtaining a manuscript to distribution of publications, along with the assignment chart for these tasks?

Appendix 2
What to consider for future publishing projects

How shall we do it in the future?

1. Make publishing part of the library strategic plan.

2. When polling public opinion, ask for your audience's opinions regarding the library's publishing activities (keep in mind that greater supplies create more demand).

3. Create a method for predicting your community's needs.

4. Evaluate positive and negative experiences so far and base your future actions on them.

5. Evaluate the potential of each library staff member to participate in future publishing activities.

6. Encourage and further educate staff who have an interest in publishing (e.g. paid internship at a commercial publisher).

7. Organise a workshop with case studies in library publishing and co-publishing.

8. Systematically inform staff involved in publishing about new trends in that field.

9. Intensify the teamwork and improve on personal relationships with experts from the parent institution.

10. Try to identify as many potential partners, sponsors and donators as possible.

11. Make sure to pay equal attention to all phases of the publishing process (once a title is published, the job is not done; in some ways it only begins then).

12. Use technological resources available for publishing activities.

13. Be sure to pay attention to the financial aspects of each publication and of the entire publishing production; include the publishing financial plan into the library budget plans.

14. Organise systematic tracking of all media coverage of your library's publishing activities.

15. Put effort into making library publishing beneficial to strengthening the role your library has in the community.

References

Bankier, J.G. and Smith, C. (2008) *Establishing Library Publishing: Best Practices for Creating Successful Journal Editors*. The Berkeley Electronic Press. Available from: *http://works.bepress.com/cgi/viewcontent.cgi?article=1014&context=jean_gabriel_bankier* (accessed 2 July 2010).

Bide, M. (2002) Adding value in electronic publishing – taking the reader's perspective. *Business Information Review*, 19: 55–60.

Blum, A. (1934) *On the Origin of Paper*. New York: R.R. Bowker Company.

Borgman, C.L. (2007) *Scholarship in the Digital Age: Information, Infrastructure, and the Internet*. Cambridge, MA: MIT Press.

Brown, L., Griffiths, R. and Rascoff, M. (2007) *University Publishing In A Digital Age*. Ithaka Report July 26, 2007. Available from: *http://www.ithaka.org/ithaka-s-r/strategy/Ithaka%20University%20Publishing%20Report.pdf* (accessed 24 July 2010).

Černy, J. (1952) *Paper and Books in Ancient Egypt*. London: H.K. Lewis.

Crow, R. (2009) *Campus-based Publishing Partnerships: A Guide To Critical Issues*. SPARC. *Available from: http://www.arl.org/sparc/bm~doc/pub_partnerships_v1.pdf* (accessed 4 August 2010).

Dumezil, G. (1977) *La religione romana arcaica*. Milano: Rizzoli.

Hahn, K.L. (2008) *Research Library Publishing Services: New Options for University Publishing.* Washington, DC: Association of Research Libraries. Available from: *http:// www.arl.org/bm~doc/research-library-publishing-services.pdf* (accessed 24 June 2010).

Hofkirchner, W.A. (2007) A critical social systems view of the Internet. *Philosophy of the Social Sciences*, 37, 471–500.

Johnson, R. and Luther, J. (2007) *The E-only Tipping Point for Journals: What's Ahead in the Print-to-Electronic Transition Zone.* Washington, DC, Association of Research Libraries. Available from: *http://www.arl.org/bm~doc/ Electronic_Transition.pdf* (accessed 17 July 2010).

Kenyon, F.G. (1951) *Books and Readers in Ancient Greece and Rome.* 2nd ed. Oxford: Clarendon Press.

Kovač, M. (2008) *Never Mind the Web: Here Comes the Book.* Oxford: Chandos Publishing.

Kovacs, D.K. (1999) Electronic Publishing in Libraries. *Library Hi Tech*, 17(1), 8–9.

Kramer, S.N. (1981) *The History Begins in Sumer.* Philadelphia: University of Pennsylvania Press.

Lowry, M. (2004) *Svijet Aldusa Manutiusa, Poduzetništvo i učenjaštvo u renesansnoj Veneciji.* Zagreb, Lokve, Izdanja Antibarbarus: Naklada Benja.

Lynch, C.A. (February 2003) Institutional repositories: essential infrastructure for scholarship in the digital age. *ARL*, 226, 1–7. Available from: *http://www.arl.org/ resources/pubs/br/br226/br226ir.shtml* (accessed 20 August 2010).

McLuhan, H.M., Fiore, Q. and Angel, J. (1967) *The Medium is the Message: An Inventory of Effects.* New York: Bantam.

Owen, P. (1996) Independent publishing. In: Owen, P. (ed.) *Publishing Now.* London and Chester Springs: Peter Owen, pp. 29–30.

Recommendation concerning the International Standardization of Library Statistics. In: *Records of the General Conference Sixteenth Session, Paris, 12 October to 14 November 1970,* Volume I, Resolutions, Paris, UNESCO. Available from: *http://unesdoc.unesco.org/images/0011/001140/114046Eb .pdf* (accessed 17 August 2010).

Renear, A. and Salo, D. (2003) Electronic books and the open ebook publication structure. In: Kasdorf, W.E. (ed.) *The Columbia Guide to Digital Publishing.* New York: Columbia University Press, pp. 455–520.

Royster, P. (2007) *Publishing Original Content in an Institutional Repository.* University of Nebraska. Available from: *http://digitalcommons.unl.edu/cgi/viewcontent.cgi? article=1133&context=libraryscience* (accessed 28 August 2010).

Saracevic, T. (2000) *Information Jungle on the Web.* Paper presented at the International Conference Information Technology and Journalism, 23 May 2000, Inter-University Centre, Dubrovnik, Croatia.

Smallwood, C. (2010) *Writing and Publishing: The Librarian's Handbook.* Chicago: American Library Association.

Svensson, L.G. and Jahns, Y. (2010) *PDF, CSV, RSS and other Acronyms: Redefining the Bibliographic Services in the German National Library.* World Library and Information Congress: 76th IFLA General Conference and Assembly, 10–15 August. Available from: *http://www.ifla.org/files/hq/ papers/ifla76/91-svensson-en.pdf* (accessed 17 July 2010).

The IFLA/UNESCO Guidelines for School Libraries (2002) The Hague: IFLA. Available from: *http://archive.ifla.org/ VII/s11/pubs/sguide02.pdf* (accessed 28 June 2010).

Thompson, B.J. (2005) *Books in the Digital Age.* Cambridge: Polity.

Urquhart, D. (1981) *The Principles of Librarianship.* Methuchen, NJ: Scarecrow Press.

Vasileiou, M., Hartley, R. and Rowley, J. (2009) An overview of the e-book marketplace. *Online Information Review*, 33(1), 173–191.

Woll, T. (1999) *Publishing for Profit: Successful Bottom-Line Management for Book Publishers*. London: Kogan Page.

Index